SIX
YEARS
IN
HELL

A returned Vietnam POW views captivity, country, and the future

Lt. Colonel
JAY R. JENSEN

ISBN 1-877898-05-8 (Paperback)
Library of Congress Catalog Card Number 89-62221

Printed in the
United States of America

Published and Distributed by:
P.O.W.
(Publications of Worth)
P.O. Box 2080
Orcutt, CA 93455
(805) 937-0869

To My Mother

Kate Pierce Jensen

Who Never Lost Hope

and to

Dad

Who Worked So Hard to

Bring Us Home

Lt. Colonel Jay R. Jensen
Author of SIX YEARS IN HELL

ABOUT THE AUTHOR

Jay R. Jensen of Sandy, Utah, graduated from Jordan High School in 1949. He joined the Utah Air National Guard during the Korean conflict and was on active duty for twenty months. Jay then attended Brigham Young University, graduating with a B.S. degree in Accounting and also a major in Banking and Finance. He attained the rank of cadet Colonel in the Air Force ROTC, and was a ski instructor and accounting lab instructor for BYU.

After working for Ernst & Whinney Accounting in Salt Lake City for five months as an Auditor, he was commissioned a 2nd Lieutenant in the Air Force. He earned his Navigator Wings in 1958, and after advanced training as an Air Electronic Warfare Officer, he was stationed in Japan, flying in the RB-66; Utah, flying in the B-57; and Oklahoma, working in a senior staff position.

On 4 January 1967, he embarked on what was to be a year of combat duty in Vietnam (Korat, Thailand). On 18 February 1967, a SAM missile struck his F-105F, abruptly ending his thirteenth "Wild Weasel" combat mission. For thirty-four months he remained on the list of those missing in action (MIAs). Then, just two days before Christmas, 1969, his family received two letters saying he was alive and a POW. On 18 February 1973, exactly six years after his capture, he was released from Hanoi in the special "group of 20" who were released as a North Vietnamese tribute to Dr. Henry Kissinger of the United States.

After his release he completed a Master's Degree in Business at BYU. Jay was recognized by five National Honorary Societies in college. He was then transferred to Vandenberg AFB, California, as a Commander of the Civil Engineering Squadron until his retirement as a Lieutenant Colonel in 1978 with 28 years service.

Colonel Jensen's decorations include two Silver Stars, Legion of Merit, Bronze Star with V for Valor, Air Medal, two Purple Hearts, Presidential Unit Citation, Air Force Outstanding Unit Award with two Oak Leaf Clusters, POW Medal, Good Conduct Medal, National Defense Service Medal with Oak Leaf Cluster, Vietnam Service Medal with 14 Bronze Campaign Medals, Air Force Longevity Award (for over 24 years), Armed Forces Reserve Medal with Hour Glass Device (20 years), Small Arms Expert Marksmanship Ribbon, Vietnam Cross for Gallantry with Device, and Republic of Vietnam Campaign Medal.

Jay has given over 600 public talks, and made eight TV guest appearances. After his Air Force retirement, he worked for Martin Marietta Aerospace for eight years and Lockheed Space Operations for two years at Vandenberg AFB on the Space Shuttle. He is a college instructor in Business Management, has taught the Certified Professional Managers Course, and is very active in civic affairs. He is a very active leader in the Church of Jesus Christ of Latter-day Saints (Mormon). Jay and his lovely wife Jan have 8 grown children, and, to date, 21 grandchildren.

This book was written entirely by Jay. It is the very personal story of his experiences, his feelings, his thoughts, his beliefs, and his hopes and dreams about his captivity, his country, and the future.

TABLE OF CONTENTS

      Jungle Survival School
      Other Survival Schools
      Korat Air Base
      The "Wild Weasel" Mission
      Equipment and Weapons
      The Missile Site Complex
      Battle Tactics

      A Beginning and Ending
      MIA or KIA?
      Thoughts to Ponder
      Pre-flight Planning
      Roscoe
      Mission Briefing
      Weasel Flight Briefing
      Personal Equipment
      Preflight
      Giddy Up Go
      Checks and More Checks
      Start Engine and Taxi
      Take Off to Hell
      The Shock of a SAM
      What Might Have Been
      What a Reception

      Torture — the Tourniquet Method
      The Hoota Hoota Meeting
      Journey to Hanoi
      The Hanoi Hilton
      Torture Again — Tied in a Pretzel
      Questions — Answers

Preface

As a prisoner in Vietnam I learned a great lesson. I learned to love and appreciate my God and my country. My hope is that by reading my account you, too, will sense this appreciation and not take for granted the freedoms, blessings, advantages, and high standard of living we enjoy in our beautiful America.

As a prisoner I suffered torture, degradation, poor food, no medical care, poor living conditions, and under the constant threat of more torture, or even death. Not knowing when, or if, we would ever be released to return home was a great stress. Would we ever see our loved ones again? The constant worry that I might be tortured to the point that I would give valuable information or propaganda to the enemy, thus dishonoring my country, or betraying my fellow POWs, was always eminent. "Home, with Honor" was our motto.

It truly was "Six Years in Hell"! A physical, mental, emotional, and spiritual "HELL." But the Lord delivered me from that hell. I was in a sense "resurrected." When I was released, it was the "first day of my new life." It was a test of faith, courage, and honor. I passed that test. "After the trial of our Faith, come the blessings," the Good Lord has said, and I have since been blessed greatly. I conquered adversity, overcame obstacles, and turned stumbling blocks into stepping stones of progress. I returned a better man than when I was shot down.

I believe that one of the reasons that God placed us here on earth is to be tested by adversity and problems. We grow and progress by overcoming these tests. Not just by enduring them but by overcoming them, by learning and progressing from them. The Lord allowed me to return in order to tell you my story. My story can help others to realize their inner strengths; to appreciate their blessings, freedom, liberty, and free agency; and to gain personal strength from sharing my experiences. These experiences build resilient personality traits such as the ability to tolerate pain, insight into ourselves, self-respect, motivation for learning, freedom to choose how we will react to events that happen in our lives, and to keep a good positive attitude and perspective of life. If I can overcome the trials I had, and keep a positive attitude, not be bitter, and be a better person for it, then you too can do likewise with your life.

My hope is that we may all gain the inner strength, faith in ourselves, and courage to face life and adversity and be "Captains of our souls," as depicted in the poem *Invictus,* by Ernest Henley, which I learned while a prisoner and that strengthened me greatly.

INVICTUS

Out of the night that covers me,
Black as the pit from pole to pole
I thank whatever gods may be
For my unconquerable soul.

In the fell clutch of circumstance,
I have not winced nor cried aloud.
Under the bludgeonings of chance
My head is bloody, but unbowed.

Beyond this place of wrath and tears
Looms but the horror of the shade,
And yet the menace of the years
Finds, and shall find, me unafraid.

It matters not how strait the gate,
How charged with punishments the scroll,
I am the master of my fate;
I am the captain of my soul.

ACKNOWLEDGMENTS

I want to thank first, my lovely wife, Jan, for the encouragement and help she gave me; also for her patience. All of my family were very supportive. Gordon Burgett was an inspiration, and gave me much needed professional assistance and advice. Deborah Worthen was extremely helpful with grammatical editing and design layout.

A special thanks for the use of seven illustrations from the book *Prisoner of War: Six Years in Hanoi* by LCDR John M. McGrath, USN. Copyright 1975, U.S. Naval Institute, Annapolis, Maryland.

I sincerely thank fellow POW, Captain Gerald L. Coffee USN (Ret.), for his POW sketches and Michele Casteel for her illustrative assistance.

I am also grateful to Rick Erickson for preparing the illustrations and photographs for printing, and Sharon Guerra for her word processing help.

Chapter One

ASSIGNMENT TO SOUTHEAST ASIA

I was a captain in the Air Force stationed at Oklahoma City, Oklahoma (32nd Air Division Headquarters, Air Defense Command) when I received my assignment to Southeast Asia in November, 1966. I was assigned as a Navigator and EWO (Electronic Warfare Officer) to fly in the F-105F. It differed from the original F-105 fighter in that it had two cockpits in tandem. I was to operate the electronic warfare gear in the rear cockpit. We were called "Wild Weasels", and our mission was to ferret out and destroy the North Vietnamese SAM (Surface-to-Air Missile) sites. We were named after the "Weasel" who is a bloodthirsty animal with a copious capacity for killing vermin. The name seemed to fit our mission very well. This is a very challenging and dangerous mission. Only very experienced pilots and EWOs were selected. The loss rate of Wild Weasels was very high at 67%.

The Wild Weasel emblem

The day after Thanksgiving I left Oklahoma City and traveled to Nellis Air Force Base in Las Vegas, Nevada, to check out in the "105". I remained there almost a month. During that time we had thirteen familiarization and simulated combat mission flights. We were paired up with our pilots. My pilot was Captain David Duart from Lafayette, Indiana. He was married and had three children. He was a very experienced and eager pilot with over

1,000 hours in the F-105. He took the mission and training very seriously and was a real "gung ho" fighter "jock".

After having completed our training we were allowed to return home for two weeks' leave before departing for Southeast Asia. We

Wild Weasels, February, 1967
Jay and Dave Duart, pilot

sold our home in Oklahoma City and bought another one in Utah, where we had many friends and relatives who would be good support for my family during my year tour in Vietnam.

We moved into our new home and settled down just before Christmas and enjoyed a very nice holiday with our three children and family. This was a very special Christmas for me, and I am afraid that we went overboard a bit in buying presents for the children. Little did I know that I would never return to that home, nor would I see my children for six long years. On 4 January 1967, I again said goodbye to my family, boarded an aircraft at the Salt Lake Airport, and flew to Travis Air Force Base, California. A few days later I departed for Southeast Asia, with a one week stopover in the Philippines on the way to Thailand.

Jungle Survival School

In the Philippines we went to jungle survival school for about a week. This was excellent training for the type of combat missions we would be flying and the type of country over which we would be flying.

At Clark Air Force Base we had briefings on survival methods, wild animals and food to be found in the jungle, and Code of Conduct. We were shown how to fill out the Red Cross form for POWs. Not much was said or known about suspected treatment of our POWs by the North Vietnamese. We were shown (in a special area) all the different kinds of snakes and also all the common booby traps and pit falls being used in Vietnam. We practiced being picked up by a helicopter and then we were taken out into the jungle to spend five days and four nights! We carried with us only what we would have if we had to eject into the jungle area of Southeast Asia (except for a blanket and jungle hammock which we were allowed to take). There was an Air Force survival expert and a local Negrito native guide to instruct us in how to travel, make shelters, and find and prepare jungle plants and food. It was amazing what that native could do in the jungle. We practiced with flares, made shelters, ate the food we had in our individual survival kits, and also what we or the native guide could find. He prepared rice cooked in a bamboo stick and roasted jungle "tubers" (sweet potatoes). We found an "imet" (water tree) and by cutting notches in it and cutting some exposed roots had an adequate supply of water. No one with a little knowledge and training should starve or thirst in the jungle.

We split up into teams of two (my pilot and me) and spent a day

3

and night on our own in the jungle to practice and simulate evading an enemy. They took us to a special area, gave us an hour head start into the dense jungle, and then the local natives were sent to try to find us. It was quite a game. We were given three tickets. Whenever we were caught we had to give the native a ticket which he could turn in for a rice supply. Well, we took off like crazy and tried to find a place to hide but the natives really knew their own area. We lost one ticket while hiding in a thicket. After much traveling up and down hills it began to get pretty dark so we just kind of gave up and made us a bed near a trail. We didn't expect them to get us at night. We no sooner got settled than here they came with flashlights. We gave them our ticket and went back to bed. The dew was so heavy it sounded and felt like it rained all night. There were many rats, and after several had crawled over my face, I just put my blanket over my head and tried to sleep. But the ground was hard, it was cold and wet, and rats kept running over us all night. It was really a miserable night.

The next morning we went to an open field. When we saw a helicopter, we shot off our flares and were picked up. We were taken to a regrouping area and a little later returned to Clark Air Force Base. We had learned a lot!

Other Survival Schools

I had previously attended three other Air Force Survival Schools, including the big month-long survival school at Stead AFB, Nevada, in February, 1959. (This school is now at Fairchild AFB, Washington). It included a week-long trek in the mountains and living a week under simulated POW conditions, including simulated torture in a prison compound situation. We also had a practice ejection seat ride on a vertical rail.

In 1959 I attended Water Survival School in Japan, which included floating in a life raft several days in the ocean and a helicopter pick up from the water.

I had also completed Air Defense Command's "Life Support" Survival School which included practicing a simulated ejection and practicing landing fall techniques from a twelve foot platform. We had three very thrilling "Parasail" rides. A parachute is put on with the chute deployed and held open by other men and a long line goes from your chute harness to a fast, powerful speedboat. You are standing on the shoreline and with the line taut, at a signal the boat takes off and you start running. You are pulled along and become airborne in a few steps. It helps if there is a slight wind blowing toward you to help keep the chute open. Of course, there is no chute problem once you are airborne. We got anywhere from 300 to 1,000 feet high with the boat pulling us all over the lake. It was really great. Then the boat would signal us and we would pull a quick disconnect lever on the line from the boat. We would then just float down to the water, pulling the handles to inflate our Mae West water wings, and simulating pulling the lanyard to drop our life raft normally attached to our chute. (In actual conditions it would pop out still attached to you by a 20–foot line, then inflate and float down with you.)

Just as we hit the water we would unsnap one riser, hopefully so the chute would blow to the side of us and not directly over us in the water. The boat would be right there to pick us up. I really enjoyed that part of our training. Parasailing has now become quite a sport.

I considered myself to be very adequately trained and prepared after all these schools. I was eager to get to our base and start flying combat. I was later to put that valuable training and experience to good use as a POW.

A few days later we flew (again by commercial jet) to Saigon, South Vietnam, for a quick stop and then to Bangkok, Thailand. On 17 January 1967, after a day or two of relaxing and a little sightseeing in Bangkok, we boarded an Air Force plane and flew to Korat Air Base, Thailand. This was to be my home for a year or until I flew 100 combat missions. It turned out to be only a few weeks.

Korat Air Base

After only a few days of getting settled and many briefings on our mission, the aircraft, rescue and refueling procedures, the base, the city of Korat, Thailand and the people, we started flying missions.

Our first combat missions were in the lower part of North Vietnam as SAM suppression and protection for the B-52s and other aircraft bombing in South Vietnam. However, we also flew several large-scale missions near Hanoi and Haiphong.

After our tenth mission we had a holiday during the annual "Tet" celebration. ("Tet" is the Chinese New Year that many Asian countries observe, so we halted bombing for five days.) During this time I attended a Latter-day Saint (Mormon) Servicemen's Conference in Bangkok and had a very enjoyable time. I was very active in our Church group in Thailand, attending meetings with servicemen and civilians stationed there. The holiday also gave me a chance to buy many presents, which I sent home to my family — children, parents, and wife.

5

The "Wild Weasel" Mission

After "Tet," the war resumed. Once again, the Wild Weasels escorted the bombing sorties into North Vietnam. A typical large-scale mission would call for a 0300 (military time of 3:00 a.m.) flight planning, and a 0400 briefing on target, tactics, refueling, weather, etc. For some unknown reason, it seemed take-off time was always about 0600 hours, and the same route was always scheduled into and out of the target areas. We would have to rendezvous and refuel with C-135 tankers both before and after going into the target area. We used to say "when the sun comes up in North Vietnam, the F-105s come in."

Our special mission was "Sam Suppression" — to locate, attack and destroy the enemy SAM sites while the other fighter-bombers (F-105s and F-4s) were bombing their military targets as directed. The "Weasels" were always the first aircraft into the target area and the last ones out! We would thus protect the other strike aircraft of about 100 Air Force and 100 Navy aircraft from the SAMs on each big mission.

Equipment and Weapons

At Korat four F-105s normally flew together on Wild Weasel missions. The lead aircraft (No. 1) and sometimes No. 3 in the flight would be F-105Fs (Weasel birds). The other two were single seat F-105s and usually carried six 750 lb. bombs. Although we could vary our armament load, normally the "F" models carried two Shrike air-to-ground missiles, and two CBU bombs. The CBU (Cluster Bomb Unit) bomb was a canister full of about 500 round baseball-size clusters containing hundreds of small buckshot-type pellets. The clusters would spread out coming down and explode on contact, giving a "shotgun" effect covering about the area of a football field. They were extremely effective on flak (anti-aircraft) sites which were around the SAM site. Sometimes we also carried an ECM (Electronic Countermeasure) pod. The ECM Pod is a canister or pod carried under the aircraft wing like a fuel tank. It contained Electronic Countermeasure equipment to jam the enemy radar of the SAM site.

In my back cockpit of our F-105Fs we had special ECM equipment which would monitor the enemy radar signals and indicate the direction of the site, the approximate range, and when a missile had been launched at us.

We also had a 20 mm "Gatling" gun or rapid firing G.E. Vulcan cannon in the nose of the aircraft for strafing the SAM site or for use against the Russian-made fighter aircraft MIGs. The Shrike missile,

6

when fired within striking range and in the direction of the enemy SAM site would "home in" on the SAM site's radar beam, following it to its source, which is a small radar van in the center of the missile site. The Shrike missile is sufficient to destroy the radar van if it scores a direct hit (which it is very capable of doing). Of course, if the enemy turns off their radar the Shrike goes "blind" or ballistic, and just continues its trajectory. However, the enemy radar must stay on in order to control the SAM missile to its target. The Shrike's impact would create a large white dust cloud around the site, making it easy to see even a well-camouflaged site from the air, and hence we could follow the missile in and attack the site to destroy the complex and all the missiles. Even a near miss of the Shrike could be very helpful in locating the SAM site.

The Missile Site Complex

The SAM missiles (maybe four to six individual missiles) are located around the radar van within about a 1/4 mile radius. The site

Reconnaissance photograph of a
Surface-to-Air Missile (SAM) site in North Vietnam

7

is usually well camouflaged (some were made to look like a village) and very mobile. Both the radar van and the missiles are on trailers and can be moved and set up again in 3 to 24 hours. The enemy radar in the van has a rotating pencil beam with a 60 nm (nautical mile) range. It locates a target (us), "locks on" to that target (stops rotating or searching and follows the target), then, when one of the missiles

Surface-to-Air Missile

around the site is launched, the radar controller remotely controls and maneuvers the missile to hit the target or as close to the target as possible. The missile has a proximity fuse. It will explode when it gets very close to a target. The missile is about twice the diameter of a telephone pole and about 60 feet long. After launch the booster engine portion falls away. That leaves a missile about 22 feet long full of very high explosives which travels at a speed of more than Mach 2 (twice the speed of sound, almost 1400 mph), with a range of over 20 miles.

Battle Tactics

Our tactics (flying in a formation of 4 aircraft) were to cruise around the target area, concentrating on areas where known or suspected SAM sites were located. In other words, we were the bait — we called it "trolling." If the radar of a SAM site "came up" (turned on and started tracking us) we would immediately turn toward the site (indicated by our ECM gear) and when in range, launch our Shrike missile and either follow it into the target or else try to get a visual sighting, so we could attack the site.

In attacking a SAM site complex, the lead (F-105F Wild Weasel) aircraft would go in first, dropping his CBU bombs and strafing in order to silence or destroy the flak site around the SAM site. This other three F-105 aircraft would be close behind to drop their bombs. It was a very effective and successful operation. Many times, when the "Weasels" (called "Iron Hand" missions) were in the area, the enemy SAM sites would not even dare "come up" (turn their radar on).

The F-105s, with a full load of bombs and fuel, however, were no match for the more maneuverable MIG 21. For this reason, if MIGs were reported in the immediate area, the F-105s would have to jettison their heavy load of bombs, abort the mission, and prepare to engage them. The F-105 was capable of speeds in excess of 900 miles per hour on the deck and could easily walk away from the MIGs. The MIG threat was a real danger to us in the Hanoi/Haiphong area we called "Package Six," as were the SAM site concentrations.

If we saw a missile launched from the ground at us or if we were able to get a visual sighting of one coming at us from a distance, it was very possible to avoid or outmaneuver the missile.

If, for example, there was only one site in the area and it was directly in front of you some distance, and the ECM equipment indicated the enemy site had launched a missile at you, there were several evasive actions the pilot might choose to take. He could make very sharp high "G" force[1] turns — "Jinking" we called it.

The pilot might just turn away from the site, rapidly changing direction, altitude, and increasing speed by using the afterburner. This would make it very difficult for the enemy radar missile controllers to correct the course of the SAM by remote control in order to intercept him. The pilot might execute a "Split S" maneuver, rolling the aircraft over on its back, pulling back on the stick and doing a half loop, (thereby reversing his original direction 180 degrees at a much lower altitude) and then by staying as low as he could, and going as fast as

---

[1]A "G" force is the pressure on your body in a turn. One G is the force of gravity. The body can stand up to about four Gs and with special G suits or partial G suits (tight fitting pants with inflatable bladders) we could stand up to about seven Gs or seven times the force of gravity. Most of you have felt these positive Gs going uphill on a roller coaster (maybe two Gs) and also going over the top you may have come up out of your seat and floated for a second, experiencing "negative Gs.

9

he could, get out of the danger area. The SAM cannot be guided and is ineffective at very low altitudes. Of course, our aircraft are highly vulnerable to small arms and 37 mm anti-aircraft fire at those low levels.

If there were several SAM sites in the area and they all "came up," our equipment would indicate the direction of each site, but it was difficult to tell which signal was coming from which site, and which site was tracking us. It was especially difficult to know which site had launched a missile at us. A tactic to use under these conditions was to "jink." While flying toward the site suspected of firing the missile (keeping the signal coming from the site just off the nose of the aircraft at the 2 o'clock position and look closely for a visual sighting of the missile coming up at you), then dodging it, or out-maneuvering it. A multiple SAM environment was a very dangerous situation. There were a total of over one hundred known SAM sites, and a very strong concentration of these was in the Hanoi/Haiphong area.

Having a battle with a SAM site reminded me of the gunfight in the movie "High Noon." I felt like the Sheriff striding slowly and very boldly down the middle of the street with his two six guns as weapons, facing an unknown number of bad guys carefully concealed in several locations with pistols, rifles and shotguns. It is quite a precarious position to say the least. Maybe that is why the loss rate of Wild Weasels was so very high. (Two out of three shot down).

Chapter Two

UNLUCKY THIRTEENTH MISSION

A Beginning and Ending

My alarm clock went off at 0230. "What a horrible time to have to get up," I said to myself as I rubbed the sleep out of my eyes. But this was no picnic, this was flying combat, and we had an important mission to fly today, number 13 for us. Strange, I didn't think of the ominous omen number 13 might be for us. I just thought, "Well, only 87 more missions to fly and then we can go home."

As I shaved with my electric razor and then showered in nice warm water, I thought to myself, "for a combat situation we have it pretty good. This is the way to fight a war. A clean comfortable bed, white sheets, a large air-conditioned (well, when it worked) room, cleaned up by a maid. A nice warm water shower and clean latrine — not bad." We had a really great Officers Club and dining hall, probably the best in Southeast Asia, and soon they would have the swimming pool completed. I enjoyed playing tennis and racquetball too.

I slipped into my flight suit and boots, hopped on my new bicycle that I had purchased a few days earlier in the little town of Korat and headed for the Officers Club dining hall. I had one stop to make, dropping a letter to my wife and children at the mail room and checking to see if I had any mail. The mail flag was flying so I knew the mail clerks had been up very late putting the mail up for us. I had two letters that I put in my pocket to read at breakfast.

As I rode past the BX tailor shop I thought, "Hey, that reminds me, I have to go into the tailor shop when I get back off the mission and get the first fitting for the two new suits I ordered. I sure do like that material I picked out, and I have been waiting for many years to get back to the Orient and have some suits custom made for me. I also wanted to pick out some Thai silk to send to my wife to make a dress. Oh yes, tonight is the time when the jeweler from Bangkok is supposed to come up to the "O" Club and bring the rings I ordered. I sure hope he has the birthstone ring for Carrie Ellen, my eldest daughter for her birthday; and the pearls for my wife, Ruth, the pretty opal ring for me; and especially the beautiful blue star sapphire ring

I had finally selected for my Mom. The family would really be thrilled about the gifts I had sent them the last few days: the rings for Ruth and the small set of bronze ware, the beautiful tapestry of the Lord's Last Supper, the Siamese dancing dolls, the small Japanese dolls for the girls, the little carved "war elephant" for Roger." Boy, there were so many more gifts and bargains I wanted to buy for my family.

As I passed the movie quonset hut I decided maybe I would go to the "flick" tonight if I got some sleep this afternoon. Since I didn't have to fly tomorrow I could go to Church, too. Well, it was going to be a busy day.

It was a few minutes before 0300 as I went into the dining room. I saw my pilot, Captain Dave Duart with another pilot, Captain Larry Waller and his EWO, Captain Jim Padgett. They were just sitting down with their breakfast trays. Jim was a very good friend of mine. We had gone to Navigator and EWO school at the same time and had been stationed in Japan together. We used to go skiing there. His pilot, Larry Waller, was very well respected and was "the" most experienced combat pilot at Korat. This was his second tour - he had flown one hundred missions and received the Silver Star on his first tour. Now he was back over as a "weasel" pilot. He and Jim had flown 67 missions so far and had "knocked out" one SAM site (for which they had been recommended for a Silver Star,) and damaged another. I was glad Larry and Jim were flying Lead in the flight today, they were pretty "cool" and an experienced team.[1]

I waved at them and, grabbing a tray, went into the kitchen. I decided I was pretty hungry so I had my favorite breakfast — S.O.S. (creamed hamburger on toast), one scrambled egg, one pancake, just a few of those fried potatoes because they looked so good, two slices of toast, jam, orange juice and two glasses of milk. My tray was pretty full.

As I sat down Dave said, "Are you sure you can handle that tray, it looks pretty heavy to me!" We all laughed. I said apologetically, "Well, you never know how long it might have to last me." I was just joking, but "fate" took me seriously. Jim said, "If you are going to eat all that we better have another game of tennis this afternoon Jay." "Great! I'm ready." I said.

The conversation finally got around to our mission for the day.

---

[1]A few years later, after two tours in Vietnam, Major Larry Waller passed away. This tragic loss of a great pilot and American fighting man and personal friend was deeply felt by many of his fellow officers as well as his family.

"What was the weather forecast?" I asked Larry, "Do you think the big 'gaggle' will go?"

"The weather is still pretty bad up North," he said, "I guess we really won't get any real big sustained missions until about May when the weather gets fairly clear in North Vietnam." Our flight was scheduled to lead a large scale mission in package six between Hanoi and Haiphong. "But we still have our back up mission down in package one," he continued.

As we ate I remembered the "100th mission going–home party" we had celebrated a few days before. It was the first one I had seen. As one of the F-105 pilots came back from his 100th mission, he received permission for a low pass over the field and was met as he taxied in by all his buddies, the ground crews, and half the base. They had a grand parade for him all around the base, then threw him in the Airmen's swimming pool and finished up with quite a party. I wondered how long it would be before our going–home party.

MIA or KIA?

We finished our meal and headed for the 13th Fighter Squadron area. As I rode my bicycle over I was thinking about a discussion a night or so before among all the "Weasel" crews. The question was, "What do you tell a guy's wife if he is shot down?" Do you say, "Yes, there is a good chance he will come back, so hang on," or do you say, "There is no way he can be alive, we watched him go in. Even if he was captured, he was probably badly wounded, might not live, might not come back for many years or never — so forget about him and start a new life." We realized, since the war had started up again after the "Tet truce," that it might last a long, long time. If a buddy is shot down, what are the chances of his being rescued, a POW, or dead? The chances of being rescued, if you went down over North Vietnam were not very good, especially in package six (Helicopters could not go north of the Red River — the risk was just too great of them being shot down.)

Because we were flying over the most heavily defended area ever known, there was not only a high probability of being shot down, but also a very high probability of being killed if you were shot down; either killed upon being hit by SAMs, MIGs or anti-aircraft or being killed by the "V" (Viet Cong) upon capture. There were very few known POWs at the time, so chances were considered slim for those captured.

Just a few days before on a mission a plane was hit. The other

13

aircraft in the flight stayed with him — watching the plane on fire, doing cartwheels end over end, until finally in a steep dive he disappeared into the undercast at about 1,000 feet from the ground. There was no sign of the pilot getting out. This happened near Hanoi, over one hundred miles inland. Everyone in the flight felt sure that the pilot didn't make it, and probably would have recommended a "presumed dead" or KIA in the official report

However, three hours later the pilot was in a hospital in South Vietnam with only two broken legs. Somehow he had managed to pull the aircraft out of the dive, had brought it under control, and had flown the very badly damaged F-105 over a hundred miles out over the gulf. He ejected near one of our aircraft carriers, was rescued, and finally flown to a hospital. His legs were broken in the ejection. Miraculous, yes, but it showed us that you never can be sure. We all decided that if there was any possibility at all of a pilot being alive, he would be reported MIA, not KIA, and we would hope for the best and tell the wife and family to "hang on" and "keep the faith."

Thoughts to Ponder

I parked my bike in front of our 13th Fighter squadron and went across the street to the pre-flight and briefing rooms. I paused and looked for a few minutes at a large impressive metal plaque on the front of the building. It said something like: We honor these brave American fighting men MIA/KIA who gave their all for their country and freedom in the World. I slowly read the long list of names that followed. Yes, many of us would not come back. This was no picnic, it was war. Little did I realize that my name would soon be on that plaque.

Why are we here? I thought. What is this war all about? Should we be here? Are we doing what is right? Is it worth the sacrifice of these men whose names I am reading now? I really didn't have time to think very deeply about it right then. However, I think all combat troops think about these very serious considerations or at least they should. I knew the North Vietnamese Communists were trying to take over all Vietnam. I knew there were millions of South Vietnamese who didn't want to live under Communism. I knew we were helping them to gain and defend their freedom. I knew that if the U.S. allowed Communism to take over South Vietnam, Cambodia and Laos, that Thailand would be next and then all Southeast Asia and Asia would be in danger, that this would jeopardize the freedom of all democratic or non-Communistic countries in the world by this

14

balance of power. Yes, I was convinced that we were there to stop the spread of Communism by force, by war, because all other ways or peaceful means of preserving this freedom had failed.

I didn't like or approve of war, of the bombing, the killing etc., but I knew it was a necessary evil. When men will not settle their differences peacefully and will not respect the rights of others then war seems inevitable.

I am a professional military man. I followed orders from my superiors. The lives of my fellow officers and the success of our mission depended on each of us following orders to the best of our ability. We did not start this war. The men who started it, the leaders of the countries involved, and the men who decided how to conduct the war and the leaders who determined and invoked those orders will be held responsible for those decisions and orders; not the men who carried them out. We were doing our duty. We were following the orders and obeying the laws of our country. It has been said, "The only time to question an order is before it's given." Certainly this is true from the military point of view. So I felt no qualms about carrying out these missions.

However, if we did not follow those orders, and unnecessarily bombed or killed people on our own accord, that would have been another story - that, in my opinion, would have been a very serious personal crime or sin that would have to be answered for by the individual.

If we very strongly disagreed with the war or the way the war was being fought from a religious conviction, moral, or a conscience point of view, then, if possible, we should remove ourselves from the position of carrying it out actively. This does not mean that you cannot serve your country, even in the military, in many ways other than combat. However, there are times in life that you have to do things you don't like to do, or don't understand the reason why you are doing them. In these cases you do them because you trust in the judgement, motives, and intelligence of those who have asked you to do those things. A member of the military knows this very well. The trust and responsibility placed with the military and governmental leaders of our nation is a sacred trust indeed. But they have more information and are in a better position than we are to see, absorb and separate all the facts and implications, and to make the correct decisions for our nation as a whole, and the world in general, both from a military andhopefully a moral point of view. Without strict discipline, respect for authority, and trust and confidence in its leaders, no war is ever won, nor cause is ever defended successfully.

Pre-flight Planning

I walked into the pre-flighting room about 0330 hours and joined Dave, Jim and Larry who came in about the same time. We checked to see what the targets were, our scheduled take-off time and refueling time and place. We decided which route into the target area we would fly and then Jim and I as the Navigators as well as EWOs preflighted our proposed mission, drawing the routes to their tanker positions and on to key checkpoints or navigational points into and out of the target areas. We figured the time over all the checkpoints, headings to take, speeds, winds etc. We noted and marked all the known SAM sites in the area we would be flying in.

Roscoe[1]

When we finished it was almost time for the big overall briefing so we went into the large briefing room. As we entered I noticed the first one to go into the briefing was Roscoe. It still seemed rather strange to me to see Roscoe. Roscoe was not a pilot or an EWO — he was a dog, a large, long-haired, tan-brown dog. He looked like a Japanese Husky. Roscoe never missed a briefing. He considered himself a very important part of every briefing. He was always the first one through the door and went right down to the front row and sat in the middle of the row. As a matter of fact he sat in the chair reserved for the Group Commander. Out of courtesy the commander

---

[1]Roscoe, the dog, was loved by everyone on the base and, indeed, he had the run of the base. He ate at the kitchen in the Officer's Club and he made regular rounds all over the base. When he wanted to go from one place to another he would hitch a ride in a truck going that direction. He knew the briefing and feeding schedules well. Roscoe liked all the men, but he would not show love or affection or get attached to any master. No one owned Roscoe, he was very independent.

Roscoe had belonged to a pilot that had been shot down (an MIA). Roscoe waited patiently many days and nights for his master to return, but he never did. Roscoe would not leave his post, he would not eat or drink. Finally one day Roscoe disappeared. Everyone thought he died of a broken heart and loneliness. A few weeks later Roscoe showed up again, almost dead from the hunger. The cooks at the Club and the guys took pity on him and coaxed him to eat. He finally resigned himself that his master wasn't coming back, but that the base was his home - just in case he did come back. He began his daily routine of attending all briefings, etc.,

had relinquished his chair to Roscoe who was the base mascot. He listened silently to each briefing and then was always the first one out of the briefing.

Briefing

The briefing started at 0400 hours. Proposed take off times were given, as were call signs to be used for the mission for each flight. Check in procedures and code names for our ground control radar sites were given. Refueling procedures, times, positions, routes etc. were presented. The specific approved targets and alternates were briefed, including intelligence reports of expected areas of SAM, MIG and anti-aircraft defenses. The ECM aircraft, including the "Weasel" flights that would be "SAM Suppression Aircraft" for the missions, were designated. All the rescue aircraft (helicopters, etc.) and ships and their locations and call signs and capabilities were briefed. A very precise "time hack" was given to us so our watches would all be synchronized. Finally, the weather, usually the deciding factor, was briefed. It didn't look good. Most of North Vietnam would be pretty well "socked in" (covered with clouds and a high overcast up to about 10,000 ft.) There was also a high wind (about 40 knots) blowing in from the Gulf of Tonkin. Chances were the target areas would be obscured by clouds and undercast from the strike aircraft. However, the mission would not be cancelled for an hour or so until the latest weather report from stations and weather recon

---

but he never was real friendly with anyone or adopted another master.

I remember Roscoe got disgusted with me one day. Several times I had driven the squadron pickup truck from the squadron area to the BOQ (Base Officers Quarters) or "Houches" as we called them, which were across the street from the Officers Club. Several times Roscoe had just come up to the truck and jumped in the back for a ride down to chow or his meal at the "O" Club kitchen. This was a habit of Roscoe's. One day I got into the truck and Roscoe jumped in too. I tried to tell him that I wasn't going straight to the Club, that I had to go another place —out of the way, over to Base Supply first. But Roscoe wouldn't get out, so I said, "OK Roscoe, come along." Well, Roscoe noted that I didn't make the right turn to go to the Club and when I stopped at supply he jumped out, gave me a real dirty look, growled a little and ran off at full speed for the Club. He never would ride in the truck again when I was driving. Sorry about that Roscoe, but many a good friend is lost by a misunderstanding or lack of communication.

aircraft was received at headquarters, 13th Air Force.

The briefing over, we completed pre-flighting and waited for the "go" or "no go" word from our headquarters. As we waited, I thought to myself, "Those old, well-worn Air Force cliches 'Hurry up and wait' and 'Stand by for late changes' were very appropriate."

We soon got the word that the main mission was "scrubbed" due to weather and we were to go on our alternate mission — "SAM suppression" in package one for the B-52s bombing down in South Vietnam.

Weasel Flight Briefing

We briefed our flight including our spare pilot. (We always had a spare crew and aircraft in case one of the four aircraft or his equipment didn't check out the last minute after engine start, tests, or during taxi, and could not be fixed within a few minutes to still meet our scheduled take off time). Take-off times had to be met within plus or minus "one" minute. This was due to the mission requirements and the large number of aircraft taking off about the same time. This being a secondary mission, take off time was slipped one hour to 0700.

Larry Waller, the flight commander, briefed our flight on engine start, taxi and take off times, explained our "join up" procedures after take off, altitudes we would fly and all the details of our mission. He explained that intelligence had briefed that there were several suspected SAM sites in package one and a few radar signals had been picked up there. The "V" might try to sneak in and set up a SAM site during the night for a one shot chance at shooting down a B-52. (Years later in 1972 there were dozens of sites in this area close to the demilitarized zone, called the DMZ.)

He suggested that if we had enough fuel remaining after our SAM suppression escort mission we would go north up the coast to Vinh and see if we could get some action out of the SAM site there. He briefed on the possibility of breaking the flight into two elements of two aircraft each, with No. 3 (us) leading the second element, if we came under attack and considered attacking a site. That way the enemy radar controlling the site could track only one of us at a time and the other element might get a chance to hit the site. We also briefed that we would not turn the ECM pods on (because we could not see the enemy radar signal on our equipment if the jamming signal were also present on our scope) unless and until a missile was fired at us; then the pilot should turn it on. We completed the briefing

18

and headed for the 13th Squadron building to get our equipment.

As I went in the building I read the bulletin board and noticed that I was still top-seeded in the squadron racquetball tournament and was scheduled to play the Squadron Commander, Lt. Col. Fitzgerald, as soon as we could arrange a match. I also noted that we were scheduled to fly again Monday.

Personal Equipment

I went into the personal equipment room to my locker. I put my wallet, bike key, and other personal articles in the locker, and put on my "G" suit, survival vest, water wings, and shoulder holster. I took my helmet and oxygen mask and went over to the P.E. counter. I checked my mask out on the oxygen equipment there and the P.E. Sergeant brought me my 38 revolver and ammunition. (We carried the pistol for protection, for possible survival in the jungle, and for use as a signaling device with tracer bullets.) I checked the gun out and then checked to see if I had all my survival gear.

Of course, there was a large, complete survival kit in the seat of the aircraft that we connected our parachute to that contained "C" rations, radio, first aid kit, one man life raft, etc. and also a paper sleeping bag in our parachute back packs; but we also carried survival gear in a special survival vest. It held such items as signal flares, smoke markers, first aid medical kit, another two way radio, and other small items. In the various pockets on my flight suit I also carried a flashlight, matches, lighter, several good knives, maps, a long rope (in case I had to let myself down from a tall tree in the jungle), some medical items, a compass, and (would you believe?) two plastic baby bottles full of fresh water. I also had a clipboard that snapped around my knee in the plane, with maps, notes, reports and mission data. We used to joke that the survival gear, chute, etc. weighed more than we did.

I slipped my parachute on, and checked out the radio "beeper" attached to the chute harness. If we ejected from the aircraft, the radio beeper would turn on when the chute opened. It would transmit continuous beeps or signals over our emergency distress frequency which could be received by any of our planes or ships in the area. They would then know we had ejected and our chutes had opened. They could also "home in" on the radio signal or by triangulation locate our position. It would continue to "beep" for about forty minutes unless turned off.

The four of us (Larry and Jim, Dave and I) went out and hopped into a squadron truck loaded down with all our gear. The driver was there waiting to take us to the flight line. The other two F-105 "D" model pilots would meet us out on the flight line.

Pre-Flight

The flight line was always an awesome sight in the early morning with its rows and rows of aircraft in their revetments (sound retaining fence), many of them loaded with their bombs; and the fuel trucks with crews just finishing fueling all the aircraft for the day's missions. It was a very impressive sight and formidable force. As we pulled to a stop in front of our aircraft, I took a long, loving look at our bird. With a full load of fuel and ordinance, the F-105 (often called the "Thunderchief" or "Thud") would weigh in at 54,000 pounds. It was built by Republic in 1965 and its maximum speed is 2.1 Mach (1,390 mph) at 38,000 feet altitude and has a range of over

An F-105F ready for action

2,000 miles. It is 67 feet long and almost 20 feet high. The cockpits, in tandem, are large and quite comfortable for a fighter, with lots of leg and elbow room. As I looked up at our aircraft, I thought, "It's no wonder everyone who flies the "Thud" falls in love with her." Our names and rank were neatly painted in large letters under each of the cockpits.

I had always liked the looks of the "Thunderchief." It really looked like a fighter — so sleek and trim, and at an angle looking coiled ready to strike. I was really thrilled and proud to be flying that aircraft. Printed on the nose gear panel was the plane's name — "Giddy Up Go."

Giddy Up Go

I liked the name and remembered hearing the song it came from. It was a sad emotional ballad that told the story about a trucker with a wife and a very young son. He took the young boy on one of his trips and his son really liked it and would say, "Giddy Up Go, Daddy" each time they would get in the big truck. When the father came home from one trip he found his wife and son gone with no trace or clue as to where, or why. Many years later, as the father was driving his truck, a really nice, new rig passed him on the highway. He followed the truck for awhile and by chance they both pulled into a truck–stop cafe. He went inside right after the young, good-looking driver of the new rig and sat down beside him. They started a casual conversation and the young man mentioned that his dad was also a truck driver. But, one day when his dad was out on a trip, his mother became ill or was in an accident, and she was taken to a hospital away from home. As a young boy he went with her. She died later, and he was given to someone else to raise and he never saw his dad again. The two men got up to leave. When they walked outside they looked at their two trucks parked side by side and on the back bumper of both trucks were the identical words "Giddy Up Go." The men looked at each other and embraced — father and son finally reunited. I am very sentimental and tender-hearted, so I liked the story.

Checks and More Checks

Dave and I checked the aircraft forms and he started his walk around inspection — checking every inch of the aircraft, control surfaces, armament, etc. I followed him; checking the items that pertained to my equipment.

Around the base we wore either fatigues or a green flight suit, but a special hat. It was a green (olive drab) broad-brimmed Australian-type bush hat with the sides of the brim snapped up. It was kind of a trademark for us. Our rank and a big Wild Weasel patch was on the front and we would put a hash mark on the hat for each combat mission we flew. As I gave my hat to the crew chief to keep until we returned from our flight, I noticed 12 marks. Only then did it dawn on me that we were going on our thirteenth mission. Little did we know that this "unlucky thirteen" would be our last. It was five minutes to start–engines–time, so Dave and I climbed the long ladder up the side of the aircraft and into the cockpits checking the seat pins, ejection handles, etc., as we got in. The crew chief, a very experienced and alert young airman, helped us get strapped in with shoulder harness, seat belt, oxygen system, radio, survival kit and all hooked up properly.

He said, "Good luck, sir. Happy hunting." I said, "Thanks, but this will be an easy mission." I checked the cold, fresh, drinking water container. Boy, that cold water really tasted good on a hot mission or when sitting on the ground for some time with the hot sun scorching you through the canopy. I was glad they put that in the "Five," none of the other fighters had it. Dave signalled the crew chief to start up the ground auxiliary power unit which was plugged into our aircraft power supply. We heard it start up and stabilize. I put my helmet on and checked out the oxygen, and then checked with Dave on the intercom radio to see if everything was okay. Each cockpit has a complete set of flight and engine instruments and controls, so the plane could be flown from the back seat (which I just loved to do). I went through my checklist very methodically, checking out each aircraft instrument and gauge and especially checking out each piece of ECM equipment to see that it was working properly. If a vital piece of equipment did not check out, or could not be repaired in just a few minutes, we would have to get out and run to the spare aircraft. We would have to quickly do our pre-flight check, and still make our take off time.

Of course, the planes flew almost every day, and the slightest malfunction was recorded and written up in detail. The maintenance crews would repair and test it. Sometimes, for a major operating item, the aircraft was flown to check it out in the air. Also the ground crews and crew chief checked the aircraft thoroughly many hours before each flight.

22

Start Engine and Taxi

I read the check list to Dave over the intercom and he would check off each item as I read it. This is standard operating procedure with two crew members to make sure nothing is missed, that every gauge is reading correctly, that every switch is in the correct position for each phase of the flight. I read the "Before Engine Start" check list. We each pushed our switch and watched as the canopies slowly closed. "Canopies closed and locked," said Dave as he hit the start button and fired it up. The powerful sound, feel, and smell of a jet engine is something only a flyer can appreciate, but 26,500 pounds of thrust (with afterburner) is a lot of power to have at your control. Dave signalled the ground crew to disconnect the ground power unit. I read the "Before Taxi" checklist and everything checked out. Dave said, "OK, old buddy are you ready to go?" "Roger," I answered, "Let's have at it."

Dave signaled the crew chief we were ready to taxi. We each held up our three seat ejection pins with their long red ribbons so that the crew chief could see them. (He will not pull the chocks away, which are holding the wheels from rolling, until he sees these pins from each of us.) He smiled, gave us a "thumbs up" and pulled the chocks from the wheels. Dave pushed the throttle forward, and the big bird slowly moved forward. As we pulled out of the parking revetment the crew chief waved goodbye, came smartly to attention, and saluted. I wondered how it must feel to him to see his aircraft taxi out, and each time wonder if it, and we, would come back.

As we were taxiing out, I checked over my ECM equipment and all the instruments, checking to see if the correct coordinates were set in the "Doppler" automatic computer navigation system. I set the correct frequencies on the radio and checked my maps, forms, etc. Satisfied, I sat back and tried to relax a little and enjoy the ride. It was very hot in the cockpit and I was already sweating, but I knew in a few minutes we would be airborne and the air conditioning would relieve that problem. Dave had checked in with the other three aircraft in our flight after engine start, and we taxied, in order, down the long taxiway to the end of the runway. We pulled into the engine run-up area in formation 45 degrees to the runway. The pilots all ran their engines up to high power while locking the brakes and checked out the engine instruments. Good, all the aircraft checked out, each checking in with Lead (Larry and Jim). Lead gave a radio frequency change and all four tuned in the new channel and checked in with Lead. There are many different preset frequencies used for each phase of a mission — radio checks, taxi instructions, tower, weather, take off clearance, after take off departures, GCI (Ground Control Intercept) radar control, airborne FAC (Forward Air Controllers) refueling, combat, emergency, approaches and landings. Lead made all the necessary radio calls for the four aircraft in his flight.

Lead got departure instructions from radar departure control (which headings and altitudes to fly immediately after take off), copied them, read them back to departure, and then we all switched to tower frequency. Lead got clearance to take the active runway. We taxied onto the main runway pulling into a tight formation. I checked my watch; it was 0659 - one minute to take off time. Lead called his flight ready for take-off and tower answered, "Roger, you are cleared for take off," and gave us wind conditions, advised us of other aircraft in the area and told us to contact departure control, which we did. The pilots all locked their brakes, ran the engines up to full power (flame shooting out the tail pipes, the engine straining eagerly) and waited for Lead's signal to release brakes and "Giddy Up Go."

Take Off to Hell

Lead raised his hand, checked to be sure his flight was ready, dropped his hand, and the four birds leaped forward as one, gaining

The F-105F in flight

speed rapidly. It was always an exciting, exhilarating feeling thundering down the runway, feeling and watching the speed build up so fast — 50...knots, 75...100...150...180. Dave eased the nose gear up. At 190 knots he eased the stick back a little more, and very smoothly we were airborne. The powerful sound of the engine faded away behind us. I read Dave the "After Take Off" check list as he brought the gear up. We picked up speed, and made a sharper angle of climb. We were gaining on the lead aircraft right ahead of us so he eased the power back, and we came slowly, but precisely, into formation just a few feet behind and on the right wing of Lead. Within a minute or two number two aircraft pulled into position on the left wing of lead and number four just behind and on our right wing. We were now in close combat fighting formation.

Departure was giving us directions: New headings, report passing through five thousand...ten thousand...and finally — cleared to in-flight frequency. We checked in with GCI radar control and leveled off at our cruising flight altitude of 12,000 feet. I was busy turning on and checking out my ECM equipment. Every few minutes after take off, at key altitudes, I called for an oxygen check on the intercom.[2]

The weather was scattered clouds, but we could get a fairly good look at the ground as we flew east toward package one in North Vietnam. Since we had a short mission we didn't need to have in-flight refueling with the airborne KC-135 tankers. The ground was a beautiful lush green because of the heavy foliage, with many small rivers. As we crossed over the Mekong River into Laos, we started getting into hills and even some small mountains, thickly forested with some high rugged rocky white "Carst" ridges. We saw very small villages every once in a while coming into view. We were alert and checking the area closely because a number of aircraft had been shot down in Laos also. The land flattened out again into a delta area, and we saw the coastline. Now we were in the very southern part of North Vietnam. We flew irregular patterns for about 45 minutes. I was busy checking my ECM scopes for any indication of a SAM

---

[2]The radio mike is inside the oxygen mask and it is an open intercom with the pilot. (We just talk normally back and forth anytime. We can even hear each other breathing.) If we want to call or answer Lead we already have that frequency turned on so either of us can just press a mike button on the control stick and we transmit to Lead. We also are automatically monitoring emergency or "Guard channel." If we want to talk to someone else we have to change or dial in another frequency. There are two separate radios in the cockpits.

missile complex. From our altitude we occasionally saw a bright flash that told us the B-52s were doing saturation bombing of roads, etc.

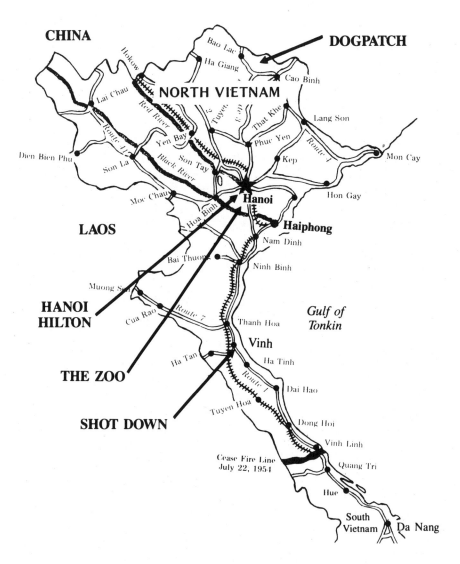

Map of North Vietnam
(Also shows location of POW camps)

When our escort mission was completed, Lead called for a fuel check. Since we all had sufficient fuel remaining he said, "Let's go North and 'troll' a little." We followed in loose formation as Lead turned north paralleling the coastline about 30 to 40 miles out to sea. As we went north the weather got worse. When we neared the Vinh area, it was solid undercast below us starting at about 10,000 feet. We were above it at about 12,000 feet. I was checking my ECM scopes and also the ground radar scope, and when we came abreast of Vinh I picked up a radar signal from a SAM site near Vinh. I pressed the mike button and reported the signal, but almost immediately the signal went down (off the air). "Well, they *are* awake this morning," said Larry over the radio. We continued north for a few minutes and then turning 180 degrees, Lead said, "Let's go back south. If they come 'back up' (on the air), we will turn in on them and try to launch a Shrike at them." We would not be able to locate the site visually and bomb it because of the bad weather, and the site knew this. They were just playing games with us, trying to sucker us within range so they could launch a SAM at us. On the other hand, we needed a radar sighting to enable us to fire our air–to–ground Shrike missiles at them or their radar van.

As we neared Vinh, sure enough, they came up. "A strong tracking SAM at 9 o'clock," I shouted into the mike. Lead had seen it too and was already turning into it. A few seconds later we got a SAM warning light from our equipment. "They've launched a SAM," we all said about the same time. Immediately Lead broke left, rolling over into a "split S" maneuver heading for the deck (ground) and going back out to sea. Number Two followed him. However, Dave and I elected to stay in there and try to launch our Shrike. Number Four must have also started to break and follow Lead, but I heard Lead say, "Stay with him, Four." We continued toward the target. Things were happening fast. In order to launch our Shrike, we had to get in range first (which we figured we were by now), and then hold a steady course, bring the nose of the plane up slightly, and then fire the Shrike. It took a little less than three seconds holding that altitude to electronically go through the missile firing sequence and for the missile to actually fire. Meanwhile, there we were, "sitting ducks" — helpless. It seemed like it took forever for that Shrike to fire. "SAM launch light still strong, radar signal very strong, a three ringer at 12 o'clock, we're pretty close to it, Dave," I said repeatedly. Dave continually needed all the info I could give him from my ECM gear. It was good to keep a little chatter going between us so we knew what each other was doing and even thinking. Finally, the Shrike launched, self-controlled and locked onto the SAM site radar. Immediately Dave broke left, pulled it down to lose altitude, and then pulled it straight and level again. "Where is the site?" he asked. "Four o'clock," I answered, "still locked onto us, still got a launch light." "Let me know when the site is at 2 o'clock," he said, as he started a

The Shoot Down

right turn. "Roger," I said and after a second or two said, "Now Dave, stop turn." He rolled out of the turn and I said, "site's at 2 o'clock, real close." I kept cross checking all my scopes and taking quick looks outside to see if I could see the SAM. We flew straight and level for another few seconds and then, Wham! We were hit.[3]

---

[3] Neither Dave nor I saw the SAM coming at us. Our wingman saw it just before it hit us. He tried to warn us over the radio, but it was too late. We never heard the call. It would have been difficult to see it because the undercast was solid up to 10,000 feet and we were about 12,000 feet so going at 1,350 mph it would take less than two seconds for the SAM to go through that 2,000 feet distance in-between the solid clouds and us.

The Shock of a SAM

What an experience. A terrific jolt and a violent explosion. The aircraft went completely out of control. I almost blacked out from the high G force. I was thrown against the side of the cockpit. There was a deafening explosion and we plummeted right through a gigantic fireball. The cockpit filled with smoke. I couldn't see a thing. I heard another explosion. I was really getting thrown around the cockpit even with the seat belt and shoulder harness tight. (We found out later, reported by our wingman Capt. Ken Curry, that the SAM had made a direct hit on the plane directly under my seat, blowing one wing off, and cart-wheeling the plane through the sky.) I frantically tried to control the stick but there was no response to the controls. I tried the radio to say we had been hit, but it was dead. I decided I had better get out fast. With all my strength I pulled the ejection handle up. The canopy ejected, and when the smoke cleared for a moment, I could see that the glass between the two cockpits was broken and Dave was still in his seat. Immediately I squeezed the ejection trigger, and the rocket seat ejected me still sitting in my seat far above the aircraft — quite a kick in the pants. I remember I pulled a lot of G's on ejection. I looked down and checked that the lap belt was released. I tried desperately to get out of the seat. But I could not get out! (It was only long afterwards that I realized that probably the reason I could not push myself out was that I was still going up at a very high rate of speed and high G force.) Finally, on the third effort, with all the strength at my command, I did manage to push myself out. My chute opened with a jerk. It was tangled in the shroud lines, but by manipulating the lines I was able to untangle them. When I looked around and found myself still above the clouds, a very lonely and depressed feeling came over me. Outside the sanctity, comfort, and security of my F-105F cockpit, I felt very, very much alone in a strange, quiet world. I said a silent prayer: "Dear God, help me. It is all up to you now. It is all in your hands. I cannot help myself much, and I certainly cannot help my family at home. Please watch over my wife, my children, my parents and family."

At about that time I went into the undercast. I remember debating whether to try using one of my radios to contact one of the aircraft in my flight and deciding that because the radio beeper attached to my parachute was emitting a distress signal already, that probably would be sufficient. (Otherwise, before using the other radio, I would have had to shut off the beeper by climbing up the risers to reach it, a difficult task at best). Next, I went through my survival procedure. I checked myself all over. I seemed to be all right, nothing broken, nothing bleeding. I checked all my survival gear. Releasing the life raft, I watched it go down and expand, attached to its lanyard. The preflight weather briefing had indicated that there was a forty-to fifty-knot wind in the area and I felt the wind blowing the inflated raft, tangling my legs in the lanyard and giving me trouble all the way down. I inflated one side of my life preserver, hoping that I was over the ocean, but when I broke out of the overcast a few moments later, North Vietnam was beneath me.

What Might Have Been

I had missed the coast by about a thousand yards and was coming down right over a village. It is strange what games fate plays with our lives. A few seconds in time and actions might have meant the difference in not being shot down, or being rescued out to sea, or being a POW for six years, or being killed.

The SAM missile launched at us was going about 2.1 mach. With a 40 knot head wind that's about 1,350 mph toward us. We flew 27 seconds after the SAM launch, with the wind that's about 800 mph. I came down almost on the coast. Therefore, if my figures are correct, if the SAM missile had been launched five seconds sooner I would have landed about two miles out to sea, or only 2 1/2 seconds sooner, about one mile out to sea, with an excellent chance of being rescued. (Of course, with that strong wind, I might have drowned, too!)

What does two to five seconds mean to you in your life? It can change your life so drastically! Just the time it takes to write your name, to take a drink of water, to tie your shoelace — in my case it meant capture and six years in hell. But back to me floating down in my parachute.

What a Reception

I looked down and could see rice fields, many peasant huts, and many Vietnamese scurrying to and fro. I think every one of them had a gun because they all seemed to be firing at me. I was certain that I would have no chance to escape and would be captured immediately —if, in fact, I landed without being killed. I heard bullets whiz by me; then one of them must have hit me, because I suddenly became very dizzy. My forehead started hurting, and my ears began ringing. I decided I had better get rid of some of my equipment so the "V" would not capture it. I pulled my pistol out and threw it away. I also broke the aerial from my survival radio so that the enemy could not use it. In an attempt to get the Vietnamese to quit firing, I slumped in my chute like I was dead. Most of them did quit firing, but by then I was almost ready to land. I was drifting directly toward a rice paddy, and not wanting to land in it, I pulled a riser down real hard and slipped my chute so that I would miss the paddy and land in some small trees nearby. I put my left arm through the left riser on my parachute and then released that riser, holding it with my elbow so that immediately upon touching the ground I could simply raise my arm to release that riser and capsize the canopy of the parachute. That way I would prevent myself from being dragged by the high winds. With my feet together and my hands crossed in front of my face, I went through the small trees, released the riser on my elbow and as my feet touched the ground I did a parachute landing roll. My feet went into a shallow trench, and some Vietnamese grabbed my hands before I could even release the other riser. I was immediately captured, and under the control of the North Vietnamese.

Chapter Three

Capture and Torture

My visit to North Vietnam was most unexpected, but what a reception! Immediately scores of screaming, hysterical peasants jumped on me. Some held me while others started beating me with hoes, rakes, and rifle butts, and tearing off my clothes and survival equipment. They didn't seem to know what a zipper was: they just tried to rip everything off me. One very old peasant woman in particular got my attention immediately. Standing about ten feet away and dipping her hand into a slimy rice paddy, she was coming up with great gobs of mud and throwing them at me — and she wasn't missing. She hit me in the face and body every time. She could have made a first-class pitcher on any major league team. I was so angry at her that I guess I forgot to be afraid of the rest of the peasants. After a few minutes some quasi-military, national-guard troops showed up. I am sure that if the military hadn't shown up, the peasants would have killed me within a few minutes. But when you think about it, their behavior was understandable. They had been bombed by our aircraft for a long time. Their homes had been destroyed, their crops and animals destroyed, and perhaps some of their family members killed. It was no wonder that they were very angry. They could finally get their hands on someone who had been doing this! However, the military, while they hated us every bit as intensely, had been instructed very carefully on how important prisoners were for information purposes and especially as barter items for a peace treaty. Their orders were to capture us alive and keep us alive — just barely.

I was stripped of my boots and most of my clothes. They gathered up my things, one man grabbed each arm, and we started running down a very narrow trail along the rice paddies. We ran and ran, away from the mob. As we ran, we would meet other peasants. I remember one old man who was hobbling down the road. He looked 140 years old, a very bedraggled man with a hoe or something in his hand. I thought we were going to run him down. But at the last moment he looked up. He didn't jump to the side, frightened; rather, he recognized me immediately as an American and attacked me. We had to dodge him to escape. We continued running down the road until finally we arrived at a very small bamboo shack. (Later on I found out that it was the home of one of the military men who had captured me). They took me inside, tied me very securely, and left me there all day. Not much happened the rest of that day. I could hear aircraft overhead and anti-aircraft guns, and I knew that my buddies were looking for me. A large crowd had gathered around the shack, and several little boys would poke sticks at me through the bamboo. If they got too close so that the sticks started really hurting me, I would growl at them and they would run away for a few minutes. They even tried to feed me a little, but I couldn't eat the food.

Late that night the crowd became very uneasy, and some military men came in and told me to get dressed, that I was moving. We went right through the crowd before they knew what was happening, and I was thrown into a jeep. We traveled for about twenty minutes. Then I was blindfolded and tied, and we started walking to another village. When we arrived, we went immediately to a main building where there was a big meeting going on. After showing me off to the peasants in that room, they took me to a side room — a very small room. In one corner was a wooden plank, evidently a bed. They told me to lie on the plank and sleep. But I was very cold. (Quite surprisingly, it was very cold in Vietnam at that time of year.) Finally they got me a blanket, and I tried to sleep, but it was too cold and the bed (plank) was too hard, and I was too nervous to sleep. After an hour or so they jerked me to my feet, gave me my boots to put on again, tied my arms behind me and took me out of the building, through the sleeping village, and down a trail or little road through the rice paddies. They did not blindfold me; I guess because it was still pitch black outside. I could only see about five feet ahead of me. I had not noticed any huts around, nothing but rice fields. One guard was in front of me and one was behind me. Both had rifles, and we were running down these little trails.

I got the idea maybe I should try to escape. We had been taught to try to escape before you got to a main prison because it would be much more difficult there. So I started running more slowly, letting the guard in front get ahead of me out of sight. The guard behind me almost stepped on my heels and gave me a little push with his rifle. I figured the guard ahead of me was quite a distance ahead by now, so all of a sudden I started really running fast — hoping to surprise the guard behind me and leave him in the dark. I was going to take a quick left or right turn at the next rice paddy road intersection, which had been every 100 yards or so. Well, just when I thought the spacing was good enough between the guards, I spotted a side road to the left, so I started to make my turn, when wham! Out of nowhere, the front guard had stopped, and I ran headlong into him, both of us falling to the ground. Both guards were screaming and shouting. They got me up and we went at a little slower pace. (Well, it wasn't the great escape, but at least I was thinking about it.)

We went to another village. Here they put me in another room. I could hear many voices outside. A little later, as it got light outside, I was brought out and displayed to the crowd, who mocked and scourged me. They were allowed to throw rocks at me and hit me with sticks. Then one of the men, who spoke rather good English, started asking me questions. I answered only with my name, rank, and serial number. According to the international code of conduct provided by the "Geneva Convention Relative to the Treatment of Prisoners of War," that was the only information we were required to give the enemy. I had long ago resolved to resist further interrogation as long as I possible could. The interrogator was asking me questions about my organization, the aircraft I flew, and other military information, which I refused to answer. I noticed in his papers two ID cards. Casually I reached down to the table in front of me and flipped one over. It was the I.D. card of Dave Duart, my pilot. I asked if he was all right. The interrogator replied that I was very lucky not to have been injured and that while my pilot had been burned, he was all right now. I had the information I wanted, but I still refused to answer their questions. This angered the interrogator, who was showing off for the crowd. He started beating me. He tied my hands behind me, putting his foot in my back, bending me back as far as he could so that he could tie the ropes to my legs. He kept calling me a criminal and a piratical airman. He said that I would be punished severely because I had not shown the proper attitude. I retorted that I was not a criminal, but a prisoner of war and demanded to be treated as such. He told me that I was indeed a criminal, that North Vietnam did not recognize Americans as prisoners of war under the Geneva convention. To them we were criminals, the blackest and darkest of criminals. We would be treated the way they would treat the worst criminal in their country. Because I had not cooperated and had not shown the proper attitude and respect, I was to be punished severely until I started answering their questions.

Torture — The Tourniquet Method

First, they put rope tourniquets around my arms near the shoulders and cinched them up tightly with pieces of wood. Then they threw me into a very dark room of a bamboo shack. There I stayed for many,

many hours. My arms immediately went numb, and my shoulders and back started hurting. Although my arms were tied behind me, I would bring them around to the side; and as I watched, they turned red, then white, then blue. I remember thinking to myself, "Gee, Jay, what patriotic arms you have — red, white, and blue!" (Little thoughts like that helped raise my spirits in those trying times).

By now my shoulders and back were really aching, and I decided that maybe if I put on a little act I might get some compassion from my captors. It was a spectacular performance, and it certainly would have won an Oscar. I moaned and groaned and tried to get to my feet. I staggered around in pain and agony, writhing in pain, and finally fainting. (At least I hoped he would think I was fainting from the pain.) But the guard evidently wasn't too impressed; in fact, he came over and started kicking me in the stomach, groin, and face, until I decided maybe I better start "coming to" before I was really hurt. So I acted as if I were just coming to. Looking up at the guard, I said, "Why do you do this to me? Why do you torture me?"

Much to my surprise he pointed outside at the crowd and said in broken English. "They make me. They make me do it." He had a compassionate look on his face, and ran out of the room. I never saw him again. In a few minutes several guards came back. But all they did was to tighten up the tourniquets. The pain in my shoulders and back was almost unbearable.

Then I began to wonder just how long I could stand those tourniquets without running the chance of losing my arms. I recalled from my Boy Scout training that it was about twenty minutes. But it had already been over twenty minutes, and the pain was getting much worse. My arms had now turned a deep purple. I knew that I had a decision to make very soon: a decision on whether it was worth trading my arms for the information they wanted.

I started to pray, and I prayed very deeply and sincerely for strength to endure the pain. Time passed. It must have been over an hour by now. I looked at my arms again, and they were black, a deathly black. The Lord had given me the strength to endure the pain.

Later, I remember feeling something hitting me in the back of the legs. I remembered that they had put some kind of a stick in the ropes to cinch them up, and whatever was hitting me felt like a stick. Wondering what it was I looked around behind me. And what I saw startled me! "They've cut off somebody's arm and tied it to me." Then it dawned on me. It wasn't someone else's dead arm, it was mine! It was a terrible black color. I realized it was now or never. I had to make the decision now. "Should I give in and tell them I will talk?" Again I prayed. I had never prayed that intensely in all my life! I asked for some kind of sign to know what to do. I prayed and prayed. Earlier I had tried to move my hands and my fingers, and as I finished praying the thought came to me. "If only I can move one little finger, I will know that things are going to be all right." I tried and tried to move my fingers and I just about gave up hope when all of a sudden my little finger twitched — just once! But to me that was the answer, the sign of what I was to do. If I had to give my arms to preserve my silence, to keep the Code of Conduct, then it was worth it. I was satisfied; that small sign had given me inner strength, and I was able to withstand the rest of the ordeal.

A long while (over four hours) later that morning they came in and released the tourniquets for a few moments. They tried to give me something to eat and drink, too, but I couldn't keep anything in my stomach. Then, for a second time, they took me out in front of the crowd and let them scream and holler. This time my interrogator had me beaten in front of the crowd. Again I refused to answer his questions. Once more he told me I would be punished until I would answer the questions. So the tourniquets went back on and were cinched up, and again I was thrown into the bamboo shack. My arms went through the same cycle — red, white, and blue, and then purple and then black. They kept the tourniquets on for about another four hours in the afternoon. (Many days later I was able to figure out how long it had been because in the shack I had been able to hear a gong sounding. The gongs were used as a communication system and timetable. The Vietnamese got up to a gong, ate to a gong at noon, and went to bed by a gong.) Finally, late in the afternoon they came in, released the tourniquets, and interrogated me again. Then they threw me back in the little bamboo shack. (It would be many weeks before I regained the full use of my arms and hands. As a matter of fact, it was almost two years before I got the feeling back in one of my little fingers.)

The Hoota Hoota Meeting

Late that afternoon I could hear a crowd of people shouting, and I knew that they were having one of their meetings. (Later we called them "Hoota Hoota" meetings, or pep rallies.) From the applauding and screaming it was obvious that they had something going on. Then they came and got me, blindfolded and tied me, put my boots on, and led me out through a field. When we were near the crowd, we stopped and waited. The crowd noise subsided, and I figured, "Well, they probably have Dave over there, and now they are going to take me over." Soon they started leading me through some fields and trees to a clearing. I could tell there were many people around, and, as I had worked my blindfold up a little bit, I could see directly in front of me; it also helped me to avoid stumbling. As we came close to the center of the clearing, I could see that they were leading me down into a depression in the ground like a gully. They were standing around the gully — I guess so that they could be taller than I was. We reached the center. In front of me on the ground was an American flag, and I could tell that they were leading me so that I would walk on it. Movie cameras were whirring, and I knew it must be some kind of press and publicity gathering for propaganda purposes. So, just as I got to the flag I suddenly dropped to my knees, leaned over, and respectfully kissed our flag.

This angered them greatly as they roughly jerked me to my feet and, with a bayonet in my back, forced me on. I could see under my blindfold that they had brought some of my paraphernalia: survival gear, life raft, and a few other things. While I was standing close to that equipment they took off the blindfold. Some interrogators, cameramen, and a large crowd were there. While the interrogators pretended to question me, the cameramen took pictures. But that lasted only a few minutes and then they marched me back to the little shack.

A short time later, when it was almost dark, I heard a very angry crowd outside. They sounded as though they were getting out of control. I was beginning to wonder if they were going to rush the place and kill me. Two guards rushed in. Excitedly they told me to dress. Not bothering to blindfold me, they kept saying in broken English, "We go fast". We went out the back door, sneaked around a little, and then ran through the fields. When they would see someone coming they would hide me. Once, as we were passing a culvert, they saw some people coming and so they had me hide under the culvert until the people had passed. My guards just stood around or wandered off a little way, which made me think, "This is a chance to escape." So, as soon as they turned their heads, I darted out of the culvert, and started running. But before I had gone more than a few feet, they started screaming at me, and I heard the bolts click in their rifles. I figured that I had better stop and not try to escape. The attempt would probably have been useless anyway. I didn't have any survival gear. I didn't know where I was or even which direction to go. And of course they were armed and were shouting at me from a short distance away. Had I tried to go farther, I am sure they would have shot me.

Journey to Hanoi

So, once more, we started running through the fields. When we finally did reach a road, there was a crowd of people after us. But around a curve in the road they threw me into a waiting truck. The truck started off and away we went. (This was the beginning of my three-night journey to Hanoi. I had been shot down over Vinh, which is only about 150 miles south of Hanoi, but we traveled only at night, holding up during the day.) After we had traveled for only a few hours, we met a small truck at a stream crossing. I was transferred to the second truck, and when I climbed into the back, I saw a 50-gallon drum of gasoline, the guards' bicycles, and amongst them, Dave, my pilot. But we weren't allowed to talk. Four guards and the two of us continued our journey to Hanoi.

One morning when we stopped, they put us in an old barn. It was very cold, so they put straw over us to help keep us warm. It helped a little. That evening as they put us back into the truck a large crowd was gathering. One of the guards (obviously an experienced orator) spoke loudly to the crowd. They started getting angrier and angrier until they became violent, advancing towards the truck and throwing stones at us. Then the truck quickly pulled away. It was all very well orchestrated for effect.

We traveled the road all that night. The road must have been badly damaged by bombs, for we took a lot of detours and went through a lot of bomb craters. Somewhere along the way, I had managed to ask Dave if he was all right, and he said that he had been burned a little on the back of the neck but was okay now. All the next day we lay in a small peasant hut because there was bombing on the road. Actually, I found the time spent in that hut very interesting. We watched a peasant woman prepare some of her meals, and I was intrigued by a large bomb shelter dug in one corner of the hut. That evening we were put onto the truck again. Another crowd of people, another arousing speech, and another rapid departure.

The Hanoi Hilton

Late in the evening — I would guess at about 2100 hours (about 8:00 p.m.) — we arrived in Hanoi, going directly to what looked like their center of the city. (Of course we were blindfolded most of the time and couldn't see much). We were taken to what we later called the "Hanoi Hilton," an old French prison where we were to spend the next few weeks. The "V" (Viet Cong) called it Hoa Loa (pronounced

Wallow), meaning "Hell Hole." I was taken directly to a torture room and interrogated; but again, I answered only my name, rank, and serial number. However, this interrogator, who told me he was the camp commander, said he was patient and could wait until I decided to talk.

Aerial view of the "Hanoi Hilton"
Prisoner of War camp

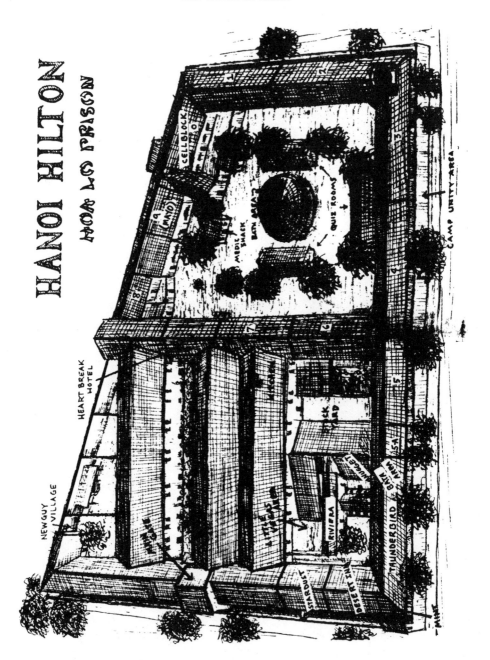

Hanoi Hilton (Hoa Lo Prison)
Sketch by Captain Gerald Coffee, USN (Ret)

At his signal some other men came into the room, stripped me down, and put irons on my hands. These irons (heavy bracelets built for smaller, Vietnamese men), didn't fit me. But the guards just screwed them down anyway — right into the blood vessels in my wrists. Then the interrogator said I would stand up at attention in that room until I decided to talk. So they stood me up and had a guard standing by. I stood at attention in that room for twenty-seven hours. (I figured out later how long it had been). Every once in a while they would come in, sit me down, and interrogate me. When I refused to answer, they would stand me up again. They did not give me food or water during this time. I had not eaten in about three days. I was sure glad that I had had that big breakfast before the flight at Korat. Finally, after about twenty-seven hours, they said that they could wait no longer. I must start answering their questions. He asked, "Are you ready to die for your country?" And when I replied, "Yes, I am, if that is how you treat POWs". He said, "Your firing squad will be here in five minutes. You will be court martialed and meet a firing squad." He then left the room. I fully expected that he was serious. I did some very serious thinking and praying then. But after a few minutes he came back into the room and said. "No, we know you are prepared to die for your country. Many men in all nations would die for their countries. But are you prepared to live for your country — to live under the conditions we will impose?" He laughed and said, "No, you cannot live under those conditions. You will talk. Normally we would just put you in irons in a cell and leave you there until you decided to talk." (And, indeed, he might have. Later I found out that many of my fellow prisoners had been in cells just as he said — alone, in irons, for days, weeks, months, and some for years.) But he said that I had information that they must know, so they would have to make me talk. Still I refused. So he said, "You are making it very hard for yourself — as you will see. You will have to talk. You won't last five minutes."

Torture Again — Tied in a Pretzel

With that he left the room and in came the big boys, the heavies — three of them. They were enough to scare any man. They had ropes, irons, pieces of wood, and everything else you might think of, and they started to go to work on me. They tied my hands behind me and put the irons on again. Only this time they weren't so careful. They screwed them, not only through the blood vessels, but also into the veins in my wrists. This hurt worse than anything else. Next they tied my feet and hands together, trussed up to my neck — in a "pretzel" —

41

One form of the "Pretzel Torture"

and cinched up on all three, strangling me! The pain was extreme, and I started screaming. So they gagged me. Then they started beating and kicking me in the stomach, groin, and face. Whenever I fell over, they would stomp on my elbow, fingers, head, and toes and give me judo chops. The pain was unbearable. They kept cinching up on the ropes and I knew that I couldn't last long. I kept thinking to myself, "Surely with this much pain I will go unconscious. Why, they do it all the time in the movies." I thought that if I could endure the pain just a little longer, I would pass out, and they would quit the torture. But, you know, it happens only in the movies. I didn't pass out. The pain just kept getting worse and worse, and they didn't stop.

I remember telling myself over and over again, "Don't give up, don't give up; hold out, don't talk." Then a very strange thing happened. As I was telling myself this, all of a sudden I heard a voice say, "I'll talk! I'll talk! Stop!" I swear it was not my voice. A very strange sensation indeed! I guess the mind and the spirit were willing but the body was weak. I found out (as every other prisoner I later talked to had found out) that their irons, their chains, their ropes and sticks were stronger than our bodies, but not our spirits.

So they stopped. And the interrogator returned and said, "So you are ready to talk now?" I said, "Yes, I'll answer your questions." By that time I think I would have answered anything. They said, "Well, it isn't that easy. You must promise not only that you will answer our questions now, but that you will answer our questions no matter when we ask them in the future. Anything we ask you to do or say. If you don't, we will bring you right back here and will torture you again the same way we are doing now. And just to make sure you remember this, we are going to continue the torture. If, in the future, you ever refuse to obey us or to do anything we ask, not only will you be tortured like this, but even after you say you will obey, we will continue to torture you." And they did continue the torture for another ten or fifteen minutes. This was the "humane and lenient treatment" that we received as prisoners of war. (I mention this treatment, not so that you will feel sorry for me, because over 90 percent of the American prisoners of war was given this same type of treatment. I mention this so you will be aware of the type of treatment that we received.) So, yes, I had to start answering their questions.

Questions — Answers

I had to fall back to a second line of resistance and start answering their questions. But I soon found that I could be very general, very misleading, and I'm confident that they gained nothing of value from anything I told them. Surprisingly, their first questions were not military questions at all but personal questions. How old was I? Was I married? How many children did I have? My family? This was the type of questions they asked. At first I was puzzled, thinking, "can they use this information against us?" We later found out that yes, indeed they could use this information against us — and against our families at home. We could lie to them about whether we were married or had children, for instance. But later, when letters came, they would show them to us and say, "But, of course, you don't have a wife or children, so you are not interested in these letters." Then they would refuse to give them to us. If, on the other hand, we did tell them the truth, they would taunt us with the letters and say, "If you will cooperate with us, if you will do and write things, and make tapes, and meet delegations, and do things like this for us, then you will be permitted to write to your family and to receive letters from them." So, they very definitely could use this personal information to our disadvantage. We were also afraid that if we were to tell them about our families and where they were, communist inspired antiwar groups would get to our families and give them a bad time. Those groups might even threaten our families or say that we would get bad treatment if our families did not do certain things for those organizations, contributing to or sponsoring them. So we were afraid of putting a burden on our families, too.

I made up stories to cover my family and didn't give them my address. However, I did give their names. Finally, they got around to the military information. When I told them I had been in Air Defense Command, they were very interested, calling in another interrogator, who was, I believe, a Russian, who asked me questions about U.S. Air Defense Command. Their first question was "How many fighter squadrons are there in Air Defense Command?" My answer was, "I don't know. I don't have any idea. I don't have information like that." But they insisted, threatening to torture me again if I didn't tell them. So, out of desperation, I asked "Well, would you believe five hundred?" "Yes," he said, and wrote down "five hundred" on his little pad.

Now I knew that they didn't know much about what they were asking for, and from then on I gave very evasive and general answers. Another question they asked was about our F-105 missions. How could we find and attack their SAM sites? What electronic equipment did we have? I said we had ten electronic jammers on the plane. They asked how they worked? I said that they had a "multi-megacycle oscillator with a push-pull amplifier and a squirrel-caged motor." This was a nonsense phrase we joked about in electronics school. They said, "oh," and made me write down every word of it. I knew then, that I could tell them anything and they would believe it. After being questioned for many more hours, I was taken to a cell — a very dismal cell — about six feet long and six feet wide, with two cement bunks, each with an attached set of leg irons. When the big iron door swung shut, the whole world closed to me. Thus I began my internment as a prisoner of war.

*A typical two-man room
in Hanoi Hilton*

Chapter 4

CONFINEMENT

It was very lonely in that cell and I wondered how long I would have to live in solitary confinement. (As it turned out, I was pretty lucky: I was in solitary for only about three months. Most of the prisoners were in solitary for anywhere from three months to a year. Half were in solitary for up to two years, and a few for four years. Of course, here — and throughout my narrative — I am speaking about the prisoners of my group, those captured in the first three or four years of the war, not about those captured in the last few months of the war or those in South Vietnam.)

Communist Standard Issue

The next day a guard took all of my old clothes and brought me some new ones, my special Vietnamese prison uniform. It consisted of two pairs of long ones, which looked quite a bit like pajamas, and two pairs of shorts with short shirts. And, because of the cold weather (I suppose), I was given an old cotton sweater that didn't begin to keep me warm. These, together with a pair of sandals ("Ho Chi Minh sandals," we called them), made of an old tire tread with inner-tube straps, were to be my clothes for the next six years. I also got a tattered old mosquito net, two very thin blood stained army type blankets, and, for a mattress on the concrete bed, a very worn bamboo mat about 1/16 inch thick. Also one very rusty old bucket (honey bucket) for a latrine.

The beds — either the concrete slabs or the wooden planks — were the hardest I have ever tried to sleep on (and as an avid outdoorsman, I have had some pretty hard ones!) I never could get used to sleeping on them. In fact, during the entire six years, I never had a good night's rest. Every morning I awoke feeling tired and sore. It was impossible for me to lie in one position for more than twenty minutes. (My poor, dear, tired wife can testify that I haven't recovered from that habit yet. I still turn over every twenty minutes.)

They also issued me a little porcelain cup, a toothbrush, some toothpaste, and (several days later) a small piece of soap that looked

Each room had its own latrine

like homemade soap (Grandma's lysol). This, I was told, was to last me for three months. It was to wash, not only my body, but also my clothes. A few days later, when I was forced to wash the dishes for my cell block, I was told that if I wanted them clean I would have to use my soap for that, too. (I ended up going almost two months without soap.)

About nine days after I arrived in Hanoi, I was allowed to shave for the first time. This was an experience I shall never forget. The blade was an old used blade that had been resharpened many times, probably on a rock. The razor itself was an old plastic one, and the blade did not fit it properly. I was not given any soap to shave with, and I had not yet received my regular soap. The only water I had was my regular cup of cold water. At Korat I had been growing a moustache for about a month. So I had a pretty bushy moustache plus about two weeks' growth of beard. That was about the most horrible self-inflicted experience I have ever gone through. When I finished, my face looked like fresh hamburger. We were allowed to shave only once a week. Perhaps that was good, as it was really torture. Every man in the cell block used the same blade. Several years later we were allowed to shave twice a week.

My toothbrush was a good example of a communist product: the handle was always breaking off. When I showed it to the guard, he would angrily scold me for not knowing how to properly use a toothbrush. When he was good and ready, he would weld the break by holding a match under it. All prisoners shared the same experience.

Some Men Died in Those Cells

The first night or so in the cell-block was quite an experience. The guards would bring us our meager meal, most of which I could not eat, and leave the dishes in the cell. I think this was to attract the rats, who used the cell as a freeway. They were all over the place. During the night I heard another POW shouting and screaming that the rats had bitten him again.

A few nights later another prisoner across the hall from me screamed and moaned for several hours. Some of us yelled as loud as we could for a guard to come. We were only allowed to learn two words in Vietnamese: "Bao Cao" (Bow Cow), which meant "report to an officer." The guard was supposed to run and get an English–speaking guard or officer.

Well, we yelled "Bow Cow" (and a few other choice American words) for a long time, but no one came to help the man in distress. After several hours he quit screaming.

The next morning they took me out to gather up the dishes in the cell-block and wash them. As I passed the sick man's room I was quite shocked. It was full of Vietnamese. There were some guards, some officers, a medic, and several women. Everyone was talking fast, very excited, and animated. The women were cleaning the room from top to bottom, even whitewashing the walls. They were talking about the night before because I heard them mimic the screams, moans, and "Bow Cows." I believe that prisoner died the night before because they would not give him proper medical attention or come to his aid.

Being somewhat susceptible to diarrhea, I had thought I would be bothered with it, but during my first few weeks I was very constipated.

The "Closet Room"

The pain was getting quite bad. After about two weeks, I was finally able to relieve myself. I determined right then that rather than suffer through that again, the next time would require a Caesarean.

I discovered that Dave was in a cell next to me, but as much as I kept trying to communicate with him, he wouldn't make contact. Finally, after a few days, I decided I would try to talk to him by speaking loudly into the courtyard through the open window during the noon siesta time. I talked with him that way for a few minutes. However, one of the guards heard us, and the next day I was moved to a new cell. I was blindfolded and led all around the camp until finally I was taken into a room, a very small room. (There were three of these "closet rooms.") This one was only three feet wide and six feet long; a very confining room. However, it did have a window at one end. Luckily, I only had to stay in this room for about a week.

The First of Many Moves

One night, after I had been at the Hanoi Hilton about a month, a guard came to my room and signaled for me to suit up (put my long clothes on) and pack up my gear. I was being moved, but to where?

I got all ready and the guards came in and blindfolded me. They led me around a bit and then, just outside the prison, they put me in a jeep. I had worked my blindfold up a little, and by lifting my head up, I could see a little bit. They had brought Dave out and two other men I didn't know. We only drove for about 15 minutes and then we arrived at a new camp.

I was put in one room for a few minutes, and then was moved to another one. I was still in solitary confinement, but what a world of difference there was between this room and the one in which I had been. This room seemed huge. It was at least nine feet wide, and about twelve feet long, with two bunks (wooden planks).

I was to find out the name of this camp was the "Zoo." It was a large camp. There were about 7 buildings for POWs and several buildings for the Vietnamese offices, interrogation rooms, punishment rooms, and even a theater. It used to be a French Movie Studio and there was even a swimming pool. But it was a long way from serving as a swimming pool now. There were fish, trash, and the remains of hundreds of "honey buckets" in it. The "V" had dumped anything and everything in it. There were 67 rooms being used for about 185 of us POWs. Later they added on an annex and put more POWs there. We figured this camp was about ten miles southwest of Hanoi.

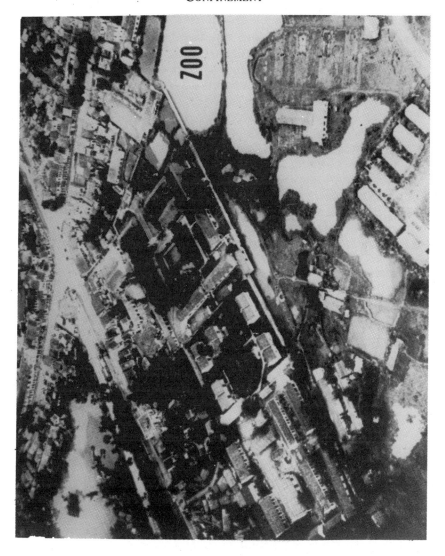

Aerial view of "The Zoo"
prisoner of war camp

Communications Were Vital

On the day that I moved in, I started hearing taps on my wall from the men in the next room, and over a period of two or three days we made contact with each other by tapping. They taught me a tap code.

They began tapping to me: one tap, two taps, three. . .to 26 taps. I understood. One tap for each letter in the alphabet. Then they sent this message: "New code," and taught me the real code. It was really very simple. The alphabet was divided into five parts with five letters in each part. (We eliminated the letter "K" using "C" instead). Each letter would be tapped in two parts. The first tap would indicate which of the five parts of the alphabet, and the next tap would indicate which letter in that row that it was.

A diagram of the code would look like this:

A	B	C	D	E
F	G	H	I	J
L	M	N	O	P
Q	R	S	T	U
V	W	X	Y	Z

All you really had to remember were the letters in the first column down: A, F, L, Q, V. You listen for the first tap, which would tell you which of these five letters it was (one tap A, two F, three L, etc.), then the next tap just continued across through the alphabet starting from the first tapped letter.

Example: If the first signal was two taps, you would think down two in the first column to "F." Then, if the next signal was five taps, you think across five from F (F,G,H,I,J): "J" would be the letter.

After doing it for some time we got very proficient at it. It was almost as fast as Morse code on a keyboard, and much less trouble to learn. The hardest part was making words out of the letters. We would have a definite pause after each word, and a series of taps after each sentence. Of course we had special signals for danger and for starting and stopping the messages. There was also a priority system for how important the message was and a classification. Most of the time we used this code we had no pencils or paper to write anything down on. Sometimes I would write with my finger and water on the cement floor.

Sometimes we could use a version of the tap code sweeping with a broom. Occasionally they would take someone outside in the central courtyard to sweep up the area with the broom. The broom was many long thin bamboo sticks tied together. We could tap by scraping the stick broom on the ground as we swept.

Another POW would use the tap code as he chopped wood each morning for a fire to boil our drinking water. The whole camp could hear him chopping the tap code. Other times we would cough, clear your throat, sneeze or any other way to send the tap code messages that were so vital to us.

I found out that we were communicating with most of the prisoners in the camp through various means. Some were very risky, some quite sophisticated. We tried many different methods: sending messages written on toilet paper with the edge of a toothpaste tube, and signaling with flash cards or hand signals. We used many types of hand signals, some right out of Cub and Boy Scout manuals. The hand signals were used very effectively from one building to another — window to window.

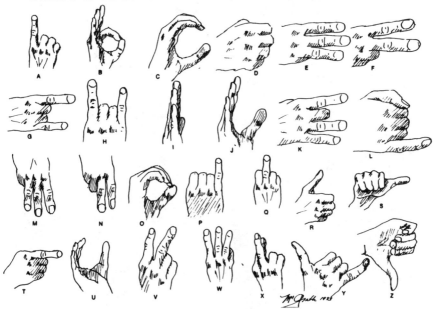

POW one-hand mute code

Another method proved very successful. We found that we could talk right through the double brick walls of our cells if one prisoner would use his porcelain or tin cup as a megaphone while the other prisoner put his ear to the same spot on the other side of the wall.

Whatever the method, though, we had to be really careful because the Vietnamese were determined to prevent us from communicating with any other prisoner in another room. They would not even allow us to see another prisoner, let alone talk to one. Once a day, if a prisoner was lucky, a guard would come and take him from the room for maybe ten minutes. He would take the prisoner outside to a small courtyard, where there was a well or cistern. There he would get one

Cup method of communicating

54

bucket of water to wash himself and perhaps have time to wash one or two articles of clothing. (Many times I had to go down to the bottom of those wells after the bucket and its broken rope, then climb back out.) Then they would go back into the room with the first prisoner and come out with the next room's one or two men. In this way we were kept from open communication.

COURTYARD –ROOM 5
of
THE "ANNEX"
Typical courtyard

Punishment

If, however, we were caught trying to communicate with any of the other prisoners, we were punished very severely. The favorite punishment they used was to make us kneel down on our knees on the cement floor, stretch our arms above our heads, and — under the threat of a guard with a rifle and bayonet in your back — stay in that position for hours, and sometimes for days. Another type of punishment used on the prisoner caught communicating (and also if they were pressuring him to make a tape or a radio broadcast, to write a letter, or to meet a delegation) would be to make him sit on a stool — just sit on a stool with a guard watching him. One prisoner sat on that stool for twenty-seven days and nights. Oh, he would fall off, but they put him right back and tied him on. Once in a while prisoners caught communicating were beaten with a hose or with the fan belt from a car. Several men took several hundred hits with a fan belt — most of them in the face. At least one man was driven insane and didn't return home. They tied bamboo mats around the legs and bodies of some men and then beat them with sticks. Because of the mats, there would be no marks left. Needless to say, we were very, very careful how we communicated. Yet, communication was vital for our morale! With it we knew what they were doing to other prisoners and were able to organize resistance. Most importantly, by communicating, we learned and memorized the names, rank, and service of every POW we knew so that if any one of us returned home, we would take the names of all POWs with us. If our names got out, there was a good chance that we would have to be released by the "V" at the end of the war.

Almost every night a series of taps were transmitted throughout the building when the 9:00 p.m. gong sounded. It spelled "G N G B U" (Good night, God bless you).

The first few weeks of capture and intensive interrogations were the worst time for a prisoner. He didn't know what to expect, was all alone, sometimes injured badly, under extreme torture, and in poor living conditions.

After the initial torture sessions, the "V" eased up a little for most prisoners unless they were pressuring him to meet a delegation, make a tape, write a confession or propaganda letter, or do whatever else they dreamed up. Then he would get the treatment I have described.

Every few months they would come up with a project to get all the prisoners to do something like read news propaganda over the camp radio, write a detailed biography, or memorize the camp regulations. Periodically, they would have a communication purge (trying to stop all communication) and many men would be tortured again as I described, or put in solitary in very small cells. If, however, you gave in to them and started doing what they wanted, the way they wanted it, without torture, you ended up being their pawn. They were then continually on your back to do things for them, as a few of the men found out.

The "V" had some strange ways of forcing us to show them proper respect. One was to force us to bow to them whenever and wherever we came near them. This was especially true if a guard came to our rooms or if we were taken before an interrogator. Those who did not bow were severely beaten until they did. We finally decided that it was better to bow than to get beaten up each time. In late 1969, however, the practice was stopped.

The Climate

Even though it was late February and March 1967, the weather was very, very cold. But when I asked the men next door what summer would be like, they laughed and said, "Our rooms get just like an oven." And they were right. It often got up to 115 degrees outside in the summer, and inside it was hotter because there was no ventilation.

The winter's cold was very penetrating due to the high humidity. Many times we would have to put on all the clothes we had and, with our blankets wrapped around us, walk back and forth in our cells, trying to keep warm. But whenever we were allowed outdoors—even though the temperature might be near freezing — we took a shower and washed our clothes. Even though we could see our breath and even though the water was almost frozen, we felt that to keep our health, we had to keep our bodies and clothes clean.

Chapter Five

KEEPING YOUR SANITY

Mentally

Those first months of solitary confinement were very difficult. How does a person keep his sanity in solitary confinement? To keep active mentally, physically, and spiritually is vital. But how does a person keep active in solitary? First, I took the opportunity to think-something that in this day and age we don't take much time to do — to sit down and think of the things I had done in my life. I was lonely and depressed, very depressed, so I tried to think positive. Recalling all the good and fun times I had enjoyed. I thought of all the vacations my folks had taken me on; all the birthday parties and picnics; outings, such as to Lagoon, a large amusement park in Utah. The hunting and fishing, camping, skiing, and especially the great deer-hunting trips my dad took me on were very pleasant memories. The many dating and courtship experiences, my marriage and honeymoon, my children — all the places we went and fun times we had — were very fond memories also.

But all these recollections made me miss my loved ones even more, and made me feel sorry for myself. I became severely depressed. To make matters worse, I then thought of the things that I had done in my life that I was ashamed of. This really made me super depressed. To be fair in this self-evaluation, I started some real introspection. I started to think of all the things I should have done, the things I wished I had done. These are the so-called "sins of omission." I was at the lowest point mentally that I could be at — excessively depressed. I felt so badly about the few things I had done wrong, and especially what I should have done, but didn't. I wanted to repent, to make restitution, to make up for those things by doing good things. But, I couldn't. My liberty or free agency to do what I wanted had been taken away from me by my Vietnamese captors. I was stopped, damned. It was HELL! It was a mental and spiritual hell, as well as a physical one. I believe that is what real hell is going to be like for all of us. That is why I called my book *SIX YEARS IN HELL*.

So I resolved to repent and change my life: to look ahead, plan, have faith in God to forgive me, and help me; to have faith in my country, my family, and fellowmen. I tried harder to communicate, and help my fellow prisoners. I contemplated what I would do when I had the chance. I tried to plan for the future. Of course I tried to keep myself entertained, too. I thought of all the songs I could and sang them to myself. I even tried to sing them out loud, but the guards complained. They didn't appreciate my singing. (But I suppose that's understandable. We didn't enjoy the singing that kept coming to us over the loudspeaker system.) I thought of books I wanted to write, and I actually outlined and wrote, in my mind, six or seven different books. (Some day I will get them all written.) I thought of talks I would give to my family, and to church groups, civic groups, and schools. I thought of trips I would take, vacations, travel to foreign lands, and I planned trips on which I would take the children.

I am kind of a nut on house plans. I love to plan homes and so I spent much time designing houses — all in my mind, of course, because the Vietnamese did not allow us such things as pencils, papers or books. Even so, I would plan the house, all the dimensions, down to the square inch. Then I would remodel it and furnish it, putting every piece of furniture in every room, and planning the color schemes and all the accessories. Then I would plan another one. I planned split-level homes, two-story homes, A-frame homes, octagonal homes, and space-capsule homes. You name it, and I tried to plan it. When I ran out of house plans, I started remodeling the homes that I had actually bought throughout my life. Then I remodeled my parents' home, my brother's home, and my sister's home.

Then I decided on sports I wanted to participate in or to watch, and hobbies I wanted to take up or continue. I planned hunting trips and fishing trips to Alaska, and safaris to India and Africa. I planned all kinds of vacations. I thought, too, about my education, trying to decide which subjects I would take, what field of study I would try to get a Master's Degree in, and which school I would attend. Did I want to be a CPA, for instance? I thought about what I wanted to do as far as my career was concerned; what advanced service schools I might like to attend, what type of job I wanted in the Air Force, and what I wanted to obtain in the Air Force as a final goal. I also planned many investments, schemes, and projects, using all the money that I hoped my wife had saved. And, of course, these schemes were all successful. As a result, I made millions — in my mind! (Maybe someday I will even try some of them out.)

What was hard on us emotionally was never knowing what was going to be next, wondering if you would be tortured into telling something that — in the eyes of some people at least — would make you a traitor, or at least disloyal. Certainly this was a big worry to me, as was the thought that I might get some disease that would not just make me ill and miserable, but leave me crippled or worse. The uncertainty, the boredom of it all, was extremely difficult to overcome.

Of course much of our time was spent thinking about how to resist the Vietnamese, particularly how to thwart their efforts to keep us from communicating, and in dreaming up ways to communicate with the men in the next room or building. We spent much of our time communicating and in helping others to communicate, warning each other when the guards came by. These are the ways that I used to keep active mentally.

Physically

To stay physically healthy, I tried — as soon as I was able — to exercise in my small cell. It had to be done without the guards knowing it, because they wanted to keep us too weak to escape or even to think of trying. So we did what we could in our small rooms, alone. Our senior ranking officers sent word through our communication network that if we were physically able we should try to do fifty push-ups and one hundred sit-ups each day. Some of the men did many more than that. Some exercised for three or four hours daily, except Sunday. A few men reported unbelievable results: 2,700 sit-ups, 1,300 squat jumps, and hundreds of push-ups.

Spiritually

How did we keep active spiritually? Spiritual strength was vital. I think spiritually is where I gained most of my strength. My faith in God, country, and family helped me to resist the Vietnamese and endure the conditions under which I was placed. We were given no *Bibles*, of course, nor song books — no books of any kind, for many years. Oh, what I would have given for the *Bible* or for other religious books — such as the *Book of Mormon!* I tried to remember all the scriptures that I could, all the *Bible* and *Book of Mormon* stories. I tried to remember all thirteen *Articles of Faith* and managed twelve. I sang all the hymns I could remember. I thought of talks I had heard and tried to remember all I could from books I had read. I did much praying. (With all that time to think over my past life and what I had done wrong, I found good cause for prayer and repentance.) Most important, I had time to ponder what was really vital in life. What were the really important things to me? They were the spiritual things. They were my Church and the principles of my Church, the commandments. As I reviewed my life I realized that without a doubt the times I had been the happiest, the most contented and satisfied, were those when I was trying to obey all of the commandments of God and being very active in my Church. Then I had known not just transitory pleasure, but enduring joy and peace of mind.

So, there in Hanoi, I decided that more than anything else in this world I wanted to be active in my Church and to obey all the commandments. I developed a greater testimony of, and faith in, my religion and became determined to live it to its fullest and to accept every opportunity to serve. To have faith in and serve God, my country (and my fellow POWs), my family, and my fellow men was my goal, oath, and creed.

Chapter Six

Superstitious! Who? Me?

As I sat in my cell feeling sorry for myself one day, I began thinking about the fact that I had been shot down on my thirteenth mission. I was not then superstitious; but later, as I began to remember other times that the number 13 had influenced my life in the preceding few years, I had a hard time shaking off some doubt. That number had entered my life thirteen times:

1. I had been married thirteen years.
2. I had completed thirteen years of active duty in the Air Force.
3. We had moved thirteen times.
4. I had received news of my assignment on November 13, 1966.
5. Thirteen days later I went TDY (temporary duty) to Nellis AFB, Nevada, to check out in the F-105F.
6. At Nellis AFB I lived in room 13.
7. I flew thirteen training missions in the F-105F at Nellis AFB.
8. Then I went on leave for thirteen days.
9. I left the States on January 4 and arrived at Korat AFB, Thailand, thirteen days later.
10. I lived in room 13 in the quarters at Korat.
11. I was assigned to the 13th Fighter Squadron.
12. This squadron was part of the 13th Air Force, our headquarters.
13. I was shot down on our 13th mission.

That is enough to make anyone superstitious! And possibly because I had become superstitious, I started thinking, "Maybe we'll be released after thirteen weeks." That didn't happen. "Well, maybe after thirteen months." I figured out when thirteen months would be up. But that day came and went, and still nothing. Next I figured out when thirteen months, thirteen days, and thirteen hours would be up. And almost to that very hour I was called to an interrogation. Needless to say, I was very excited. And the "V" officer, whom I had never seen before, was also animated. He said that he had some important news for us. (My heart skipped a beat.) President Johnson had stopped the bombing in North Vietnam! I was really excited-for awhile. I thought for sure that we would be going home soon. (But "soon" was to be four and one-half more years. The next thought I hardly dared contemplate: "Could this mean it would be thirteen years before I went home?")

Chapter Seven

PRISON LIFE

Solitary confinement was hard on me, but I soon became accustomed to the boring routine of prison life. The highlight of the day was a chance to communicate with the men next door. By peeking out through a crack or a little hole in the door, we could see a little of the courtyard and the rest of the prison. Observing other buildings and the rooms and men in my building, I soon realized that Dave was right next door to me, although I could not get him to answer my taps. However, the men in the room on the other side of me told me the names of many men in my building and in other buildings, the number in the camp, and many other important items. Finally, after a few months of solitary, I was put into the next room with Dave.

It was a relief to be out of solitary and to have a roommate with whom to talk. A few weeks later, Dave and I were moved to another building and were put in a corner room, and after a few days Captain Joseph S. Abbott came to live with us. Having three of us in the room was much better.

Joe was from Alloway, N.J., married, and had seven children. He was a very devoted family man. He had been the Flying Safety Officer at his squadron in Thailand and an F-105 pilot.

Dishpan Hands

The three of us did the dishes for the rest of the building. But we didn't really mind this extra work because it gave us another chance to be outside for a few minutes each day. The guard was pretty mean and never smiled. (Of course, neither did we.) On our first day of dishwashing, I remember, when he was showing us how to get water from the cistern to do the dishes, he dipped some water out of the cistern and, going swish, swish, threw the water over his shoulder. Much to everyone's surprise, the water just missed another guard who was standing very close. The guard screamed and ran off. We three thought that this was pretty funny and burst out laughing. For just a moment the guard smiled and started to laugh. But then he got his angry look again. As a matter of fact, he went and found the other guard and showed us that he wasn't really wet. (As I look back, I realize that it was the first time I had laughed since my capture. It felt kind of strange.)

Hot as Hades

By now the hot, humid summer had arrived, and most of the prisoners, including me, developed medical problems. The biggest problem, I guess, was heat rash. The extreme heat — up to 115 degrees — together with the cramped conditions, really aggravated that heat rash. We were almost all infected with extreme jock itch or ringworm. The only medication they gave us for it was iodine. Your can imagine how it felt to put iodine directly on those sores and directly on the very delicate and personal parts of our body. It burned!

Each day in Vietnam, from about noon to one o'clock, was quiet time. Everyone would take a siesta — everyone, that is, except us. From 1:00 to 3:00 p.m. (during the heat of the day) we would work in the yard, doing heavy shovel work and weeding the garden. We felt we probably should do this work. The guard said that the vegetables would be for the prisoners. I developed heat blisters all over my body. They would swell up until they were about as big around as a half dollar and about one-half inch high with fluid underneath. Then they would break and get infected. I developed heat blisters all over my body. My roommates would kid me, saying that I had leprosy and that they didn't want anything to do with me. (Perhaps they really thought I did!) The guards would do nothing. We kept asking for medical help. Finally, I became desperate. I yelled and yelled until an officer came and looked at me. He called a "medic" who took me out on the porch and very obligingly poured iodine on all those open sores. The guard that had shown us how to wash dishes stood by and laughed at my pain, but the next day or so he disappeared. Apparently his behavior had cost him his job, because for the next few weeks we saw him on KP detail, and he had been demoted in rank. Several years later he was still working in the kitchen and held the same rank.

After a few months, Dave was moved to another building, which left Joe and me roommates for the next two and one-half years. Joe and I got along pretty well. I loved to talk and Joe didn't mind listening — for a little while.

Chow Time

The highlight of our day was always chow time. We ate two meals daily — one in the morning, and one in the afternoon. The food was not what we were used to. As a matter of fact, I had real difficulty learning to eat Vietnamese food. But, I decided that if I were going to survive, I would have to "learn" to eat their food.

At first the only thing I could eat was the rice. It wasn't like American rice, it was very bland and not very filling. We could eat and eat the rice, but an hour later we would be hungry. So we would have to go to bed hungry. The rice contained pieces of bamboo, dirt, rocks, and a few other things. The rocks in the rice shattered two of my teeth. During the first three years our diet consisted primarily of rice, soup,

Prison eating utensils

and a side plate of some kind. (Part of the time we got bread instead of rice.) The soup we called "weed soup" or "sewer green soup." It was a greenish substance in hot water and had leaves and little twigs or branches! I didn't mind those I could get down, but when they were big enough to be tree limbs and stumps — I couldn't quite swallow those. It tasted vile. At first it made me sick, so I tried to eat it a little bit at a time. The first day I would try one spoonful; the next day, two; the next three. But then I would get so sick that I couldn't eat for two or three days and would have to start all over again.

In the wintertime we had cabbage soup. I never was able to get used to that soup. It always gave me diarrhea. The side or extra plate usually contained the same things that were in the soup — weeds or, sometimes, cabbage or turnips or kohlrabi. Once in a while we would get a little pork fat or side fat. Not much meat on it! There usually was just a little black speck with the fat: hide and hair attached. Once in a long, long while we would get soy bean cake (TOFU), sometimes in the soup, sometimes even fried. Eventually it became my favorite.

Once in a long while, too, we might even get some fresh carp. It was terribly bony, but it tasted pretty good. We had dried stinky fish sometimes. The Vietnamese ate them bones and all. Some of the prisoners were able to eat them that way, but I usually spent quite a bit of time trying to get out the little bones without losing what little meat there was. This was our usual diet for the first three years. Sometimes, though, we got a surprise. I put my spoon into the soup one day, and much to my surprise, I found a delicious treat — the head of a chicken. Later, when I asked the Vietnamese interrogator about it he told me that I had been very lucky. The choicest morsel — the cock's head — was always given to the family patriarch at a big family feast. But I am afraid I didn't appreciate that particular custom. Sometimes we would find a chicken foot (with toenails) in our soup, too. Once a dead rat was found in the soup bucket.

Prison Pets

We had lots of little pets around the cells. I have never seen so many rats in all my life. And some of them were as big as a small dog. We could see the rats through our cell window. They could climb trees like the best monkeys I have ever seen. They could climb a barbed wire fence and I have seen them go straight up a ten-foot brick wall without any trouble at all. They entered and left our cells at will through the ratholes placed in every cell block. We could hear them in the attic day and night. I believe they ran North Vietnam, especially at night. Many nights I awoke with a rat crawling over me or taking a bite out of my ear. Oh, what a horrible feeling that is to wake up to!

The mosquitoes were very bad also. I have never seen so many mosquitoes as in the swarms that entered our cells each evening. This

67

was especially bothersome because the Vietnamese would not allow us to put up our nets until 9:00 p.m., about two hours after they swarmed. I have never had so many mosquito bites. One morning Joe and I decided to have a contest to see how many mosquitoes we could kill with our bare hands, just catching them in the air, not against the wall. In a very short time each of us had killed several hundred.

The cockroaches were the biggest I have seen. Some of them must have been a thousand years old. There were many bugs and ants and, oh yes, the lizards-the little geckos. They were our favorite pets. They would come into the rooms at night and climb up the walls. We liked them because they liked mosquitoes. One little gecko used to come in every night and get on top of my net and catch mosquitoes. He was young and wasn't very good. As a matter of fact, he usually missed about three out of four. But one night I watched him catch and eat over two hundred mosquitoes, so he was learning. Once in a while a gecko would take on a large moth and a battle royal would take place. The gecko usually won.

We saw several snakes in the area, some of them poisonous. Later, at the camp in the mountains, we killed two very poisonous ones right at the foot of my bed. I even stepped on one in the middle of a pitch black night. That was quite a thrill.

My Greatest Worry

I suppose that my greatest worry as a prisoner was that I would be forced to give information, or make statements that might embarrass my country or make me look like a traitor. For that reason I considered myself fortunate that I had not been injured. Men who had been injured or wounded or who had been hurt severely from torture were in a very precarious position because the Vietnamese took advantage of their condition, denying them medical aid to get them to do things. Because of the primitive conditions and the filthiness, any medical problem could be very serious, even a minor cut, bruise or cold. I was susceptible to sinus trouble and was afraid that I would get a bad spell of it in this climate. And, sure enough, when the Vietnamese were trying to get me (along with everyone else in camp) to write a detailed biography, I developed a very bad cold and sinus condition, and had unbearable migraine headaches. In fact, the side of my head swelled up to about twice its size. I kept asking the Vietnamese for medicine and they kept refusing. After several days of steady headaches and no sleep I was called in to an interrogation (or "quiz" as we called it). On the interrogator's desk were five or six different types of medicine, among them aspirin and tetracycline. He asked me if this was what I needed for my sinus problem, and I said, "Yes, I think that is what I need." Then he said, "Fine, as soon as you complete your biography you may have the medicine." I protested, and so he ordered me back to my room. The next day he called me back. Finally, after this procedure for another week, when I could stand the pain no longer — I wrote the biography, and he gave me the medicine. This problem was magnified many times for those seriously wounded.

A Visit with Fred

Once when the guard had brought Joe and me back into our room after we had done the dishes, he closed the door but failed to lock the padlock. This was just too good an opportunity for me to resist. After a few minutes, when the guard still hadn't shown up, I carefully unlatched the door, opened it, and (with Joe watching for the guard) tiptoed down the hall to the next room. There were small one-foot-square doors in each room door. These were held with only a latch so that the guard would not have to undo the padlock to talk to the prisoners or to give them food and water. I unlatched the little door, banged it open (just as the guard would have done), and shouted, "Fred!" Fred jumped up, very surprised and excited. "You scared me to death," he said. (Major Fred Cherry, our building's SRO (Senior Ranking Officer), had been in solitary confinement for several years because of his admirable resistance. And he had been injured severely under torture. In addition, he had been given three major operations, under barbaric conditions.) When I asked Fred how he had been feeling since his most recent operation, he showed me his thirteen major scars and said, "Not well." We talked for a few minutes, Joe gave him some gum and cigarettes, and then I went to the next room and talked with another prisoner for a few minutes. Soon, however, we heard a guard coming, and so we rushed back to our room without being caught. It had felt great to talk with other prisoners.

Talking With Neighbors

After many months the other rooms established the cup method of communication with us, and then we spent much time talking to the adjoining rooms through the walls. Besides discussing the problems at hand, we talked about personal things and sometimes tried to entertain each other, telling jokes, stories and relating movies. I asked the men in the next room about their religion, and when they had finished, I told them about mine. Day after day I told them about Mormonism through that double brick wall. All kinds of information went through those prison walls: religion, sports, girls, plans for the future, school.

Even so, the hours and days seemed to drag by very slowly. However, the weeks and months and even the years seemed to pass very rapidly. It is said that we remember only the good things in life. Perhaps that is why those months and years went by so fast — there wasn't anything pleasant to remember.

Chapter Eight

CHRISTMAS COMES TO HANOI

That First Christmas

It was December, 1967, and was getting very cold again in Vietnam. One day we heard some very strange, but familiar noises in the courtyard: "Gobble, gobble, gobble."

"Joe, I hear turkeys!"

"Turkeys? Oh, come on!"

But there were turkeys. About twenty in the central courtyard. And we saw and heard those turkeys until Christmas Day. They sure made a racket, and they sure made a mess. We had heard that they were going to be given to the prisoners for Christmas. The Vietnamese promised many things for Christmas: a wonderful meal, decorations, church and even Christmas music. We wondered just what Christmas would be like in a Vietnamese prison camp.

Have you ever been away from home on Christmas? Away from your loved ones and family? More or less all alone in a strange place, perhaps a strange country? If you have, you may understand what I mean when I talk about how lonely you can be at Christmas. Throughout most of the year, we heard Radio Hanoi almost every night over the speaker installed in each cell. In fairly good English, "Hanoi Hannah" would broadcast propaganda to the prisoners and to the troops in South Vietnam. The only news we got about home was all the bad news. Anything antiwar, anything catastrophic that happened in the United States, we would hear about that. But then, around Christmas time for perhaps an hour a day, we heard all the old familiar Christmas tunes and carols. All the wonderful tunes that made us homesick: "I'll be Home for Christmas, If Only in My Dreams" or "There's No Place Like Home for the Holidays" or "Peace on Earth Good Will Toward Men." Oh, how we wished for that "peace on earth."

The Vietnamese put colored lights up in the courtyard and decorated one room with a Christmas tree and homemade decorations. On Christmas Eve they took one room at a time to see the decorations. I will have to admit it did remind me of Christmas, but I am sure that they used it for propaganda. Afterwards the camp officials met each

71

group of prisoners in another, smaller room. On this one day of each year, they would be very pleasant, wishing us a Merry Christmas and expressing the hope that we would be home for Christmas the next year. They would even offer us a little piece of candy or a cookie or a cigarette. And then we were taken to a little room decorated with a Christmas spirit, complete with an altar and candles. With a smug look, the Vietnamese officer said, "We have decided that on Christmas Eve, once a year, you may come to the room, kneel at the altar, and pray to your God." (What a joke! Once a year they were going to allow us to pray! I just smiled and said, "I don't need your altar or your permission to pray. I can pray any time I wish — anywhere.")

The Vietnamese also said that prisoners would be allowed to attend church service on Christmas Eve. There would be one church service for Catholics and one for Protestants. I told them I was neither and didn't desire to go. I felt that it would be just a propaganda effort, and I was right. Those who attended the service said there were more photographers and cameramen than prisoners. Because of all the movie cameras and flashbulbs, it had been impossible to hear the preacher.

We ate the turkey for Christmas, and I would say that with what the Vietnamese had, it was the best meal they could prepare. But they had a budget of only so much money each month. So, to give us a special meal they would have to cut down on their budget for several months in advance. As a result, for many, many days before that special meal we almost starved to death. Of course, it made us appreciate that meal much more. On one other day each year we got a good meal. They celebrated Tet, the Chinese New Year; and on that day, too, we had a really good meal. This meal consisted mainly of what they called "bangchung," very tasty stuffed meat rice cake. Sometimes they would even give us half a bottle of beer, which was supposed to really help us. I don't drink, but my roommates enjoyed it.

Christmas 1968

A few months before Christmas Day of the second year, 1968, the guards came into our room and said that we would be allowed to make a Christmas present for each room of prisoners. We would be allowed to make paper or cardboard chess sets. We didn't really believe they meant it, but we decided to go along anyway. So we spent about a week making a chess set. Using cardboard and other things that they had given us, we made little three-dimensional figures. Then we decorated them with aluminum foil (from cigarette wrappers and such) and painted half of them black (with paint the Vietnamese had supplied). The finished product was very nice, and the Vietnamese agreed. But they told us that we would have to make sixty-seven more in just the few weeks left before Christmas. It was obvious that at the rate we were working we would never finish, so we had to make the sets a little cheaper and not put quite so much work into them. We did manage to finish by Christmas, and they actually did give them to the prisoners. Each room got a paper or cardboard set and the prisoners were very glad to get them. Joe and I felt good about being able to give a useful present to all the other POWs.

The True Meaning of Christmas

What did I miss at Christmas? I missed Christmas decorations, Christmas carols, stories, TV, and the traditional Christmas food, I missed the giving of gifts, the parties, the Christmas cards and letters, the news we got from friends and relatives at Christmas time, the family get-togethers on Christmas Eve, the children. What is Christmas without children? Oh, how I missed my children! I longed to be seeing what Santa Claus had left them, watching them play with their Christmas toys, taking movies of them. I missed visiting the relatives Christmas Day; and, being from Utah, I missed the white Christmas. How I missed the snow and mountains and skiing during Christmas vacation. But most of all, I missed the church services and the stories of Christ.

I thought about the true meaning of Christmas: the Savior's birth, the tradition of giving. He gave us peace on earth, good will toward men (oh, how we longed for that). He atoned for our sins. He gave us His wonderful teachings, His gospel plan, His love, His example to show us the way. I remembered the story of the Garden of Gethsemane, where Christ prayed and sweat blood from every pore. I thought how I could appreciate that much more now, because I had left my blood, sweat, and tears on the torture room floor.

Chapter Nine

LIFE GOES ON, AND ON, AND ON

The Motorcycle Story

A story went around the prison grapevine that Jerry Venanze, a prisoner, had a motorcycle. Of course, he was just pretending he had a motorcycle. (To avoid having to do things for the enemy, several men pretended that they were a little crazy. And Jerry was an expert). He kept his motorcycle in his room so that the "V" wouldn't steal it. And each day, when he was taken out for his ten minutes, he would wheel his cycle out, start it up (complete with sound effects), and ride it wherever he went. He washed, polished, and repaired it regularly, too. Jerry even pretended he had a friend who lived with him, a little South Vietnamese boy whose parents had been killed by the Viet Cong. The boy went everywhere with Jerry, riding on his motorcycle.

At first, the enemy didn't know how to handle the situation, so they ignored it. Finally, though, the act got to be too much for them. The camp commander called him in and told him "I'm sorry, but you must not ride your motorcycle around the camp any more." Because they didn't have motorcycles to give to all the prisoners, he explained, it was unfair for Jerry to have one. So Jerry started walking. However, a few months later, they moved us to a new camp, and Jerry was seen wheeling his bike and putting it in the truck with him.

Ask a Silly Question

Another favorite POW story is about a Navy pilot who was being tortured severely for information. But as regularly happened, he did not have an answer because there wasn't an answer. The "V" wanted to know the names of all the pilots on board his aircraft carrier who had refused to fly combat missions against North Vietnam. I think they had read in some American paper or some of their American "friends" had told them that many American pilots were refusing to fly combat because of their opposition to the war. Well, one of the weaknesses of the Communists is that they believe their own propaganda. They had been told by their superiors to come up with some definite names of pilots.

Well, the poor POW didn't know any names, because no pilots on his ship had ever refused to fly combat. He kept telling his torturers this, but they wouldn't believe him and kept increasing the torture. Finally, out of desperation (and many of us reached a point where we would say anything, just to get them to stop), he decided to make up some names. So he said "Well, yes, there were a few pilots who refused to fly. There were Captain Marvel, Captain Dick Tracy, Clark Kent, and a flight surgeon, Dr. Ben Casey."

The "V" really bit on that information. They did not question it at all. As a matter of fact, I understand that they publicized these names all over the world at a big Anti-War Conference in Japan or at the War Crimes Tribunal in Sweden. Finally, someone wised them up that they had been had — royally.

Of course, they came back and took it out on the POW. He was treated pretty badly and put in irons and kept in solitary for several years. They told him that nothing they could do to him could possibly make up for the harm and embarrassment he had caused the Vietnamese people, but they would try. Well, ask a silly question, you get a silly answer. The "V" just have no sense of humor!

Nighttime

Most of the time we had a small 20-watt bulb in our room that burned all night long. This was so that the night guards could come around every little while, bang down the little hatch on our door, and check to see if we were still there. We got used to sleeping with the light on.

Usually when it rained really hard, however, the lights would go out, and would be out for some time — maybe days. The thunderstorms in Vietnam were some of the worst I have ever seen. We called it rolling thunder and it would thunder from the tip of South Vietnam clear up to China it seemed.

Other times the light bulb might just burn out, and they may not change it for a while. But, when the light was out — it was dark, and I mean pitch black in those rooms. It reminded me of the poem "Invictus."

> *"Out of the night that covers me,*
> *Black as the pit from pole to pole. . ."*
> (see Preface)

Well, this darkness was nice to sleep by, but it also caused a few problems. Because of the extreme heat in the summer, we drank all the

75

water we could get, plus the soup, and this meant that we had to get up sometimes three or four times a night to relieve ourselves. Our "honey bucket" was in a corner. But to navigate in the pitch blackness from your bed to the corner and even find the bucket was quite a chore, let alone making sure your aim was good and you hit the bucket. Finding your way back to bed was no easy task either. You could get vertigo really easy.

One POW told how he was in a great hurry one night to find the bucket in the dark, and just barely made it to squat over it. The next morning he woke up, looked around and then burst out laughing. Over in the corner on the lid of the bucket sat a very picturesque monument to his nocturnal episode. He had forgotten to remove the lid in his haste.

Another story concerned two POWs who were in a room together and both had been injured with broken legs and had very heavy casts on their legs. (That was typical Vietnamese logic to put two men together that couldn't walk or help each other out very well.)

Luckily they had two buckets and kept one under each bed at night so they wouldn't have to find it because it was very difficult on crutches. Well, in the middle of the night nature called for one of them. He adjusted the bucket at the side of his bed, lifted up the mosquito net with one hand and tried to complete the operation without getting all the way out of bed. But he lost his balance at a critical moment, fell out of bed on top of the bucket, knocking it over with him right in the middle of it. Wow! What a mess!

Camp Regulations

On the inside of the door of every cell was a copy of the camp regulations. Failure to comply with any of these regulations was an excuse for punishment, solitary, or torture. But the rules and regulations were so unreasonable you couldn't help but break several every day. The old regulations were especially bad, and were worded in poor English. In early 1969 they revised the regulations so they were not quite so ridiculous. They also came out with a program that each POW had to memorize the new regulations.

The new regulations were dated February 15, 1969, and stated, "In order to insure the proper execution of the regulations, the camp commander has decided to issue the following new regulations which have been modified and augmented to reflect the new conditions. From now on the criminals must strictly follow and abide by the following provisions:

- The criminals are under an obligation to give full and clear written or oral answers to all questions raised by the camp authorities. All attempts and tricks intended to evade answering further questions and acts directed to opposition by refusing to answer any questions will be considered manifestations of obstinacy and antagonism which deserves strict punishment.
- The criminals must absolutely abide by and seriously obey all orders and instructions from the Vietnamese officers and guards in the camp.
- The criminals must demonstrate a cautious and polite attitude to the officers and guards in the camp and must render greetings when met by them in a manner already determined by the camp authorities (bow). When the Vietnamese officers and guards come to the rooms for inspection or when they are required by the camp officer to come to the office room, the criminals must carefully and neatly put on their clothes, stand at attention, bow a greeting and await further orders. They may sit down only when permission is granted.
- The criminals must maintain silence in the detention rooms and not make any loud noises which can be heard outside. All schemes and attempts to gain information and achieve communication with the criminals living next door by intentionally talking loudly, tapping on walls or by other means will be strictly punished.
- If any criminal is allowed to ask a question, he is allowed to say softly only the word 'bao cao.' The guard will report this to the officer in charge.
- The criminals are not allowed to bring into and keep in their rooms anything that has not been so approved by the camp authorities.
- The criminals must keep their rooms clean and must take care of everything given to them by the camp authorities.
- The criminals must go to bed and arise in accordance with the orders signaled by the gong.
- During alerts the criminals must take shelter without delay; if no foxhole is available, they must go under their beds and lie close to the wall.
- When a criminal gets sick he must report it to the guard who will notify the medical personnel. The medical personnel will come to see the sick and give him medicine or

send him to the hospital if necessary.

- When allowed outside for any reason, each criminal is expected to walk only in the areas as limited by the guard-in-charge and seriously follow his instruction.
- Any obstinacy or opposition, violation of the preceding provisions, or any scheme or attempt to get out of the detention camp without permission are all punishable. On the other hand, any criminal who strictly obeys the camp regulations and shows his true submission and repentance by his practical acts will be allowed to enjoy the humane treatment he deserves.
- Anyone so imbued with a sense of preventing violations and who reveals the identity of those who attempt to act in violation of the foregoing provisions will be properly rewarded. However, if a criminal is aware of any violation and deliberately tries to cover it up, he will be strictly punished when this is discovered.
- In order to assure the proper execution of the regulations, all the criminals in any detention room must be held responsible for any and all violations of the regulation committed in their room.
- It is forbidden to talk or make any writing on the walls in the bathrooms or communicate with criminals in other bathrooms by any other means.
- He who escapes or tries to escape from the camp and his (their) accomplice(s) will be seriously punished."

Code of Conduct

It is very interesting to compare the *USA Code of Conduct of the American Fighting Man* with the "V" list of regulations. You can see they conflict:

Code of Conduct

1. I am an American fighting man. I serve in the forces which guard my country and our way of life. I am prepared to give my life in their defense.
2. I will never surrender of my own free will. If in command, I will never surrender my men while they still have the means to resist.
3. If I am captured, I will continue to resist by all means available. I will make every effort to escape and aid

others to escape. I will accept neither parole nor special favors from the enemy.

4.   If I become a prisoner of war, I will keep faith with my fellow prisoners. I will give no information nor take part in any action which might be harmful to my comrades. If I am senior, I will take command. If not, I will obey the lawful orders of those appointed over me and will back them up in every way.

5.   When questioned, should I become a prisoner of war, I am bound to give only name, rank, service number, and date of birth. I will evade answering further questions to the utmost of my ability. I will make no oral or written statements disloyal to my country and its allies or harmful to their cause.

6.   I will never forget that I am an American fighting man, responsible for my actions, and dedicated to the principles which made my country free. I will trust in my God and in the United States of America.

The Code of Conduct was an outgrowth of studies made after the Korean War to strengthen the American fighting man — to let him know what was expected of him, and to give him a code of ethics or honor. However, in some areas, it is very general. We found that there were many circumstances not covered specifically enough in the code. Some areas were not covered at all. For instance, on surrender, would you, with only a pistol, fight it out to the end against a hundred "V" soldiers closing in on you from all sides? And what is meant by the "means to resist" capture?

It brought to mind the situation of one of my roommates. After his shootdown, he was hiding behind some rocks with the enemy all around searching for him. He had contacted American aircraft on his radio and a "chopper" was on its way. He had seen many of the enemy in the immediate area. All of a sudden, into the clearing, came three enemy troops. Well, actually they were three young boys about ages nine to twelve. The biggest boy had a rifle as long as he was. Then one of the boys spotted and pointed at him, too scared to yell. The boy with the gun holds his ground and slowly points his rifle at the American behind the rocks. OK, what would you do? The code says, "I will never surrender of my own free will. . .while I still have the means to resist," You have a pistol pointed at the boy with the rifle. You could probably kill him and maybe the others too. But the shots would bring a hundred enemy Vietnamese to you in a moment. What do you think they would do to you after they captured you and found you had shot and killed the boys?

He didn't shoot the boy. For when he looked at the young boy, he saw his own son about the same age in his mind . He just couldn't do it. Could you? Instead he threw his gun out toward the boys, raised his hands, and made three more young boys Vietnamese heros. What does it mean to "resist by all means?" What does it mean to "evade answering questions to the utmost of my ability" (except name, rank, etc.)? What is the utmost of your ability? Does that mean never? Does it mean after torture? How much torture? What kinds of torture? Mental torture? Threats of torture?

We had some pretty good arguments on what was a "special favor from the enemy." Was special food (a little better or different food) a special favor, especially when you were sick? What if the guards brought around something different like extra cigarettes, a banana, an orange, a grapefruit, cookie, or candy and just gave it to you or dropped it in your cell and left. Should you take it? Should you eat it? Or would that be a special favor, since you didn't know if the other POWs in the camp got any?

If they brought in a book, or pencil and paper, or paper and water colors to paint, or took you outside and told you that you may stand in the sun, or play ping pong, or volleyball, or exercise, and you knew that all of the POWs were not allowed any of those privileges, was that a special favor? If they told you that you would be allowed to write home because of your good attitude, and you knew only a very few POWs in the camp were allowed to write, should you go ahead and write? If they said, "if you write a letter to the Camp Commander and apologize for your past actions and promise on your word of honor you will faithfully obey all the camp regulations, then you may write home for the first time in three years," should you do it? Or if they said, "If you will meet this American peace delegation visiting Hanoi and give the right answers to this list of questions, then you may write a letter home and they will take it with them," should you do it? Or is that a special favor? Or if you were tortured to do the same thing, then, is it OK? How much torture?

Do you write down the words to an American song from a tape? Do you transcribe a tape of an American nationwide debate on the war recorded from an American TV set? Do you transcribe a tape of anti-war leaders that was played on American radios? Do you read the propaganda newspaper over the camp loudspeaker system? Do you write a letter about a trip your building of POWs took to a museum in Hanoi? Do you write a biography on yourself? Do you write a peace

80

plan proposal to end the war? Do you do any of these things? Do you do them if they threaten you? If they put you in solitary? If they torture you? How much torture should you take? What priority system should exist for what kinds of information? There were so many questions and situations not covered by the Code of Conduct.

To begin with, you were on your own almost completely when in solitary. You made your own decisions. If you got another cellmate, and he was a higher rank, he then interpreted the code. We tried to get communication with other adjoining rooms and set up a system to receive specific instructions from the building SRO (senior ranking officer) or the camp SRO. We had to interpret the code as it applied to us in those circumstances, which were very different than in Korea. We made our own regulations ("plums", we called them). We passed these to new men as soon as possible. We set up a priority system. Some things you could tell under slight pressure, other things under torture (physical pain), other things only under significant unbearable pain, and others were not to be told under any circumstances.

We tried not to accept anything even resembling a special favor until we were assured that all would receive it. If that was not possible to determine, we accepted it the first time, but not again until we knew all had received the same.

Some men questioned the Code as being binding on them. Was the Code just a goal to strive for like an honor code at a college? Was it a service regulation, or a law? What would be done to me if I didn't live up to it?

Most American POWs (I would estimate 95%) tried to the utmost of their ability to live up to our *Code of Conduct*. This included being subjected to extremely painful and enduring torture. I am sure many of those that did not come home were tortured to death trying to live up to the Code. But while some gave their lives, and others were tortured and lived in solitary and irons for years trying to keep the code, there were others with lower levels of resistance. There were some who resisted a little, but when it started hurting, decided to talk. When the "V" just verbally threatened them with torture, a few believed them, gave in, and did what they asked, perhaps trying to make what they wrote inaccurate, misleading, etc. And then there were a few who made no effort whatever to resist, but did what they were asked to do from the start. And perhaps there were also a few who not only cooperated but collaborated. Nine men were released early, some of these only after a few months of captivity. We do not know why or how. I will not judge these men! The "V" could have picked any one of us. Whether we would have gone, I don't know. But I do know the "V" interrogators held these men and their statements and letters up to us as examples. We were tempted with, "If you will cooperate and show a good attitude to the camp authorities, you, too, may be rewarded by going home early." I said, "No thanks, I have to live with myself."

What should be done with the *Code of Conduct?* Some changes were made and clarified because of this war as with any war.[1]

Life Under Communism

In Communist North Vietnam we learned that the quality of everything was usually very poor. Sometimes (as with their cigarettes) they would make a cheap product and one of better quality. Everyone in Vietnam knew which brand was the best. Sometimes the best brand was not available, especially at the one and only people's department store in Hanoi. The brands on the wrappers were not for advertisement (because the government made all commercial goods), but were propaganda or patriotic sayings. One brand, for instance, was Dien Bien Phu.[2]

The "V" could never understand why we couldn't tell them which brand of cigarette, or car, or toothpaste, or soap was the best one in

---

[1]In November, 1977, the following changes were made in the official *Code of Conduct.* Article V had said, in part: "When questioned, should I become a prisoner of war, I am bound to give only name, rank, service number and date of birth."

President Carter, on the advice of a Pentagon report on the code, replaced the word "bound" with the word "required" and eliminated the word "only." This sentence now reads: "When questioned, should I become a prisoner of war, I am required to give name, rank, service number and date of birth."

The report said, "Some ex-POWs stated that [their] training did not prepare them adequately for their ordeal and left them with a feeling of guilt when under extreme torture and duress, they divulged more than name, rank, service number and date of birth to the captors."

Carter agreed and said the change would provide a more uniform understanding of the code and eliminate feelings of guilt.

[2] Dien Bien Phu, close to the Laos border, was the scene of a great historical (7 May 1954) and decisive battle between the French occupationists defending their very heavily fortified stronghold and Vietnamese troops under Ho Chi Minh. This disastrous defeat of the French ended the "Vietnamese war of liberation" and led to Vietnam independence at the Indochina armistice 21 July 1954 at Geneva.

America. We would say they are all good — very good. It was just a matter of personal preference, color, taste, etc. They could not believe why we had such soft beds,or large houses with luxuries such as furniture, TVs, radios, washing machines, dryers, etc. They accused us of being wasteful and extravagant, while millions of Americans died of starvation every year, and the minorities lived in poverty. They didn't realize that our poverty level is a higher standard of living than anyone in Vietnam will ever know.

North Vietnam made only the necessities of life, nothing else. They had one steel plant (courtesy of Russia), one small tractor factory and that's about all the industry. A few watches, radios, and motor-cycles were all imported, mostly from Japan or North Korea.

Of course, all their war materials and weapons, to speak of, were from Red China and Russia.

We were told, and read in some of their books, that a typical peasant family (90% were peasants) would have to pay for their own family's medical needs, schooling, clothes and any luxuries (such as if the family had a water buffalo). They would work on the commu-nity-owned rice paddies to get just enough ration of rice to live on. They might have a small 1/8th of an acre lot beside their bamboo hut to raise a few vegetables, chickens, etc., to sell and get money for their medical needs, school, material for clothes, etc.

In the city, however, the emerging new "worker" who joined the Communist party and union, had social security benefits in old age, free medical care, free schooling. If he was really lucky, he had enough money to buy a bicycle for himself. The very few who were chosen to go on past a basic education not only were competing for the highest grades but also they had to be very active in the Communist Party Youth Organization.

They had elected officials in their government, and they held elections. However, they only had one political party — the Commu-nist party. Therefore, almost all the elected officials were commu-nists. No other political parties were allowed. They did manage, however, to elect a member or so from each of the minority groups, even one from a church group, just so they could say they were truly a democratic republic. The elected officials, in turn, then elected men to the highest offices in the land.

It was interesting that all the people are required to attend patriotic/political meetings (we called them "Hoota Hoota" meetings) three or four nights every week.

They were very much interested in American products and our ways of doing things. We had a few interrogators who would ask a great many questions about the USA. Of course, they would never believe us when we would tell them quite honestly about our homes, cities, clothes, automobiles, sports, etc.

All of the interrogators (who were usually Vietnamese officers) could speak English quite well. Then they had one guard (an NCO) over each building in the camp. He could speak fairly good English. He was what we called the "turn-key" because he had the keys to all the rooms in the building and would be in charge of that building. He would take each room out to wash, pick up their food, take us to quizzes (interrogations), etc. They also had other guards who would patrol inside the camp and were security guards. These men (of low rank) could not usually speak any English.

Our Captors

We called one "V" officer the "Rabbit" because of his big ears. (His ears from the side view were shaped just like a question mark.) He thought he was really hot stuff, and used to ask us about going out with girls on dates (because in Vietnam the boys went with boys and the girls with girls mostly). He asked if there really were shows where girls danced without clothes on, and Playboy clubs, etc.

We called another Vietnamese "the Lump" or "Lumpy" (because of a lump on his head). He was the assistant camp commander at the camp we called the "Zoo." He was actually the Communist Political Commissar of the camp. He was always in civilian clothes. He played the role of the good guy. He never directly asked you to do anything or punished you. I had several quizzes with Lumpy over several years. He asked a great number of inquisitive questions about life in America. He was especially interested in camping out, camping equipment, trailers, all kinds of campers, etc. I asked him why he was so interested. He finally told me that when the war was over he wouldn't have a job, and so he was preparing himself for a government position as head of the North Vietnam Tourist Agency. He said millions of tourists from all over the world would come to North Vietnam after the war to see their famous country and they would have to prepare for them.

We called one officer the "Sheriff" or "Ivan, the Terrible." We called him the Sheriff because every time you had a "quiz" with him he would end up telling you to put your hands up high, and stand on your knees.

The most hateful guard was "Pox." He was thin and had many pox marks on his face. He was the meanest, cruelest guard I knew. The

*A typical North
Vietnamese guard*

guards in the camps were all hand-picked. They had to be very faithful to their country, well disciplined, and hate Americans. Many were chosen, (a "V" officer told me), because someone very close in their family had been killed or wounded by American bombing. Most of them were sadistic, cruel, barbarous, brutal and megalomaniacs. A very few showed any mercy or humaneness at all, and none showed friendliness.

The most intelligent Vietnamese I met was an interrogator we called "STAG," (because he was "Smarter Than the Average Gook"). Stag was raised in South Vietnam, as far south as you can go. As a young boy he was a "cowboy." That's what they call the boys that ride the "cows" (water buffalo). Then he was a spy against the French and now he had moved to the north. He was a very intelligent and dangerous man. He could speak five languages.

"SPOOK"   "RABBIT"   "SPOT"

Other Vietnamese guards

85

Another Roommate

In about April of 1969, Joe and I got another roommate, "Spike" Nasmyth. Spike was quite a character. For a little while I didn't know whether Spike and I were going to get along. He is the only POW I knew who claimed to be a confirmed atheist. I used to kid him that he was really just an agnostic. But we got to know each other and had some interesting discussions. One of Spike's old roommates was A. J. Myers. A. J. had access to an English dictionary for a short time and had memorized quite a list of words and their definitions. He had passed these on to Spike, who could remember many of them. Spike passed them on to us, and when A.J. moved in next door to us, we could talk to him through the wall.

Solitary Confinement

Shortly after Spike moved in with us the "V" started a new campaign to get many different POWs to read the "news" over the camp radio. They would not read it live, but would tape it, and then if the "V" were satisfied they would play the tape over the camp radio. Several men were tortured or placed in solitary over this. Some were making the news tapes too. We received word to hold out if possible; but don't take too much torture — then go ahead and read it, but try to goof it up.

We were called to several quizzes and asked to read the news. I kept telling them no. About the third time they said because of my bad attitude and influence I would be punished. They put me in solitary about the first of April in 1969. The small cell was in the rear of the theater building. The room was fairly small but not bad. The worst part was the millions of mosquitoes that swarmed into the room from a big hole in the ceiling that went into the attic of the theater. Every night it was really bad for a few hours until the guard would let me put up my net at 9:00 p.m.

I was interrogated two or three times a day and threatened for several weeks. The second day that I was there was the first Sunday of the month, I remember. That day is called "Fast Sunday" in my church. (We fast for two meals, give the money saved to the poor, and then attend a special "Fast and Testimony" meeting). I had been fasting for some time by not eating one of the two meals we received on that Sunday, so I told the guard or tried to tell him I didn't want to eat that one meal. Well he either didn't understand, or else he thought I was crazy, or he thought I was rebelling against the camp authorities.

Not only did he take the food back, but I didn't get offered any food for two days! I tried to get to talk to an officer to explain, but they just ignored me for a few days.

After about a week some of the food must have been bad because I got terribly sick to my stomach with real bad pains. I "Bow Cowed" and screamed for a officer, for a medic, but no one came to do anything for three days. I thought I was going to die from poisoning. Finally, when I could hardly walk, I was taken to a quiz and a medic checked me and gave me some pills.

After about a month the "V" said he had been too easy on me and if I would not agree to make the news tape he would have to punish me. I told him he already had. He put me on my knees with my hands high up in the air and stationed a guard behind me with a gun with a bayonet to poke me if my hands came down. Every once in a while I could cheat a little when the guard left for a minute (a short minute). That lasted about three hours that morning. They took me over to my cell for lunch. I was really beat. My knees were swollen and bleeding. The muscles were really sore and knotted up, and my back was really aching. I thought, boy, is it worth it, should I give in? I got to my sore knees and prayed about it. I received the strength I needed. I received this same torture every day for about two weeks. I got pretty weak. Finally, one Sunday, I decided I couldn't stand it any longer and was ready to give up at the next session. I prayed for confirmation from the Lord and help to endure the pain.

I was thinking to myself it just wasn't worth the torture when all of a sudden I couldn't believe my ears. There was organ music — and singing coming from a nearby building. American voices, good voices. I listened carefully; it sounded like a tape. No, it was too clear. I recognized the song now; it was unbelievable. They were singing loud and clear now. The whole camp heard a choir singing, "The Lord's Prayer!" I was stunned. How about that for a direct answer to my prayers. It gave me the courage and strength to continue resisting. I found out later it was a group of men in the camp led by Quincy Collins that the "V" had allowed to sing once in a while. They sang for a POW church service on Christmas. I was very grateful to Quincy and the boys that day.

Movie Time

The next morning was quite a change. No quiz. Instead the "V" got ready to show a movie in the theater. They set it up so they could bring one room at a time over to the theater and sit them down in a space surrounded by blankets hung as a divider so they couldn't see any other POWs in the theater room. There were no seats; we sat on the floor, and it was dark inside. I watched through a little peephole in my door and got to see almost every man in camp walk right in front of my door. What a treat that was, to see all those POWs close up. Then one of the guards opened my door. He was with the traveling film group, and he smiled and said in broken English, "You will be allowed to see movie today. Put on long clothes." While I put on my long clothes (in the 110 degree heat) I thought, "Now isn't that just like the 'V.' One day they torture you, the next day you see a movie." The movie guard said, "Do you like to see movie?" I answered, "Yes, it is much better than standing on your knees all day!" He gave me a puzzled look and took me into the theater.

I can't remember what one of the movies was, maybe the usual newsreel showing their glorious victories in the south, where a 12-year-old boy hero kills his 100th "yank" with pungi sticks and stolen American hand grenade mines. But the main movie was the best we ever saw there. It was a Russian film of the Moscow air show. It was really interesting.

After the movie I went back to my solitary room and I thought, "that's a lot different than the movie we saw last Easter." We were told that we would receive a big meal, church services, and a movie for Easter. Well, the meal was a little better than usual and then we went to a movie. The movie was the most blood-thirsty, horrible thing I have ever seen. It showed supposedly bombed areas, homes, bodies, arms, legs, heads, people with CBU pellets in them, deformed babies, and you name it. I just didn't think that was the way to celebrate Easter. Vietnamese newspaper accounts reported that while American planes raided North Vietnam the American POWs enjoyed a wonderful banquet, special movies, and church services for Easter.

I found out later one or two POWs did go out and meet with a Vietnamese Catholic Priest who gave them communion. It is also interesting that he "granted them absolution from all their sins, including 'hideous war crimes' against North Vietnam."

The Escape

After the Russian movie it was "back to work" and torture as usual. Shortly thereafter, sometime in May, 1969, there was a really bad rainstorm, and the lights went out. This wasn't unusual. But, early the next morning, the guards in camp were very busy. Guards checked to see if I was still around about five times. Others were running all over the camp.

From a peephole in my door, I could see the front gate of the camp and the row of buildings that were the prison officers' quarters. I had spent many hours a day looking through that little peephole watching the activities of the camp. But I had never seen so much activity as this morning. There were Vietnamese all over the place, running here and there, talking and shouting very excitedly. There were also a dozen or so very high ranking "V" officers in the area.

A little later the front gate opened, and I saw two Americans brought in. One was dressed in a brown outfit and the other in black. They were blindfolded, hands tied behind them, and the "V" were running them towards me and being pretty rough. At first I thought it must be some new POWs. But then I figured, no, not in those clothes. Yes, there had been an escape.

This was the second escape I had known of. I didn't know any details about the first one except he was gone some time but caught. It would be very, very difficult to escape from the camp in the first place. Then you would be in the middle of Hanoi and the densely populated surrounding area with millions of very short, dark skinned people everywhere. Where would a six-foot, white American hide?

The two men were Captains John A. Dramesi and Edwin L. Atterberry. They had escaped during the previous night's storm. They had been caught the next morning, their freedom short-lived.

The "V" put the men in separate rooms; one was put across the courtyard from me. I watched the guards and the "V" officers go in and out of his room all day and night. For the next 24 yours I listened helplessly as the screams of terror echoed from that room. I could hear them beating him all that day and through the night. The next morning it continued. There were still many "V" civilians in the camp, the women who cooked, etc., and guards running around very excitedly. I noticed the camp medic pacing up and down in front of the escapee's room. He actually seemed very upset and distraught.

A guard went into the prisoner's room carrying a basket full of something white. Shortly thereafter, the POW started screaming, "No, no, not that." I heard them hit him, and the screams were muffled after that like they had gagged him. About ten minutes later, the guard came out with the basket. At the same time the guards took me out of my room to empty my honey bucket. The torturer came right by me, and I saw that the basket contained salt. It was like a rock salt, the same kind they gave us occasionally with food. But I never did figure how they used the salt to torture the man (who I think was Atterberry). They could have put the salt on some open wounds or else maybe made him drink salt water, but I don't know.

By afternoon the screams stopped. That evening the "V" had an especially big, noisy, very heated debated "Hoota Hoota" meeting. I remember some of the women were really verbose and excited, and sounded like they were really telling somebody off. No one ever saw Ed Atterberry again. We all believe he was beaten and tortured to death for escaping. Dramesi said he was beaten and tortured severely for 30 days after his recapture, and then harassed for an additional six months.

There was much retribution in the camp over the escape. Many men in the annex were questioned, beaten, put in solitary, etc. There was a crackdown camp-wide. Windows were bricked up, security tightened, and the guards got meaner, if possible. Many items such as medicine, sugar, chess sets — anything like that — were taken from all the POWs. I was sent back to my old room with Joe and Spike shortly after this. I had been in solitary about six weeks this time.

Man's Best Friend

The North Vietnamese had some rather strange and cruel customs. For instance, it was well known that they ate dog meat. In fact, it was quite a delicacy for them. They would go through quite a ceremony to prepare this special feast. When the little puppy got the right size (big enough, but still young and tender) they would have a big celebration. They would all get in a circle around the puppy so he couldn't get away and then stone and beat the dog to death. Several times we heard and saw this horrible scene, and heard the yelps of the tortured dog. Even after it was dead, they beat it some more — I suppose to make it tender. Then they had a special way of preparing it for the meal, roasting it in its own juices for many hours.

It was said that in South Vietnam you could sometimes tell if a recent campsite had been Viet Cong or South Vietnamese by digging around the fireplace for bones. If you found dog's bones it was Viet Cong because the South Vietnamese didn't eat dogs. Yes, man's best friend in North Vietnam was also man's best meal.

North Versus South

But whether they eat dogs or not is not the only difference between the North and South Vietnamese people. From North Vietnam's own literature I learned much about their country and attitudes. They tried very hard to give the impression Vietnam was one country, one people, united against tyranny. They had been fighting for their independence for four thousand years against enemies who had been trying to conquer their small, valiant, but strategic country. We used to describe it as their "4,000 years beside the rock" pitch. They fought China for 1,000 years or so, although most of this time they were occupied and ruled by China. However, Vietnam never admitted being conquered or defeated. But the truth is, even during these thousands of years there was always a Northern part or principality and a separate Southern part. It is true that China has coveted Vietnam because of the rich, overabundant rice-growing resources. As a matter of fact, I believe the Vietnamese are still more afraid of China taking over or dominating their country than anyone else in the world. They are very careful and wary in dealings with China. China, on the other hand, politically, would prefer to keep Vietnam as a cooperating communist buffer state.

French colonization and domination over all of Indochina, including Vietnam began as early as 1787. It was continuous until World War II. Following the surrender of France to the Germans in 1940, Indochina gradually came under control of Japan. Japan left control nominally in the hands of the Vichy regime of France, but fostered the growth of nationalism. In March, 1945, having interned the French Vichy administration and troops, the Japanese proclaimed the autonomous State of Vietnam, with Bao Dai, emperor of Annam, as ruler. This puppet state collapsed after the surrender of Japan. But France wasn't in a position yet to reoccupy Indochina. At the Potsdam Conference the Allies agreed that Nationalist Chinese would occupy north of the 16th parallel and British troops south of it until the French could resume control. But on 22 August 1945, the Viet Minh League led by Ho Chi Minh, a communist, proclaimed the creation of the Free Democratic Republic of Vietnam. This led to a long war.

France reestablished itself in Vietnam, and British and Chinese forces withdrew. Ho Chi Minh headed a war of independence against the French until his victory at Dien Bien Phu 7 May 1954. Armistice agreements signed at Geneva set up a provisional military demarcation line along the 17th parallel, with the northern territory going to the Viet Minh under Ho Chi Minh (now and from then on the greatest hero in Vietnam), and the South under control of the Saigon government, under Bao Dai. Under the Geneva agreement, elections were to be held in 1956 for a unified government in Vietnam. In 1955, however, Premier Diem sponsored a referendum in South Vietnam ousting Bao Dai as Chief of State. He proclaimed South Vietnam a republic, proclaimed himself president, and refused any election talks with North Vietnam.

91

One of the big arguments used by the Communists was that the present conflict with the USA was a continuation of the war of independence with France. They had tried to unite all the people of Vietnam against the US or any foreign power in order to gain true independence and be one Vietnam. Of course, this would mean one Vietnam under communism.

One day an interrogator was pointing out to me how bad conditions were in Saigon compared to how great Hanoi was. He pointed to a news article and said, "Look what you Americans have done to Saigon. Look at the problems they have — 20,000 taxi drivers in Saigon have gone on strike for higher wages. It is causing much trouble in the city."

I looked at him and shook my head. I said "Saigon has 20,000 independent taxi drivers who are free to join a union and strike for higher wages and standards of living. How many taxis are there in Hanoi, and what would happen in Hanoi if your people organized and went on strike against the government?"

He looked very puzzled and finally said, "We don't have any taxis; we don't need them, and the people would never strike because they are so happy with what they have. Now that is all. Go back to your room!"

Well, it is true that Ho Chi Minh was a great man (although politically communist-oriented). He did a lot for his country. The French did little for Vietnam except exploit it. For instance, they were still exporting half the rice crop while millions of Vietnamese starved to death. According to Vietnamese publications, they had trained only one doctor in all of Indochina after almost 200 years of sometimes very brutal colonization.

Economically, the communist system could do much to raise the standard of living in a country such as North Vietnam in a very short time. Like a peasant said, "Before Ho Chi Minh I had nothing, my family was starving to death. Now I have everything, thanks to Ho Chi Minh." By "everything" he meant he was not starving and had clothes and shelter. He didn't know what he *could* have. He didn't know what the South Vietnamese have, or the Japanese, or the rest of the world, and he never will — his Communist government will see to that. It is quite easy to make rapid advances in a country when you start out with nothing. But their progress will go only up to a certain point, a point we or other countries would consider below our lowest level. This includes nothing but the very basic items available. The government runs and owns everything. They set and control production, distribution, and prices of all goods. There is no competition; therefore, there is no quality, no need for advertising, no inflation, and no overspending. The government completely controls all news, radio, communications, publications, education, and transportation. Food is distributed to all who will work. There is no unemployment because if you don't work you don't eat. It's very simple.

When the Communists took over, they confiscated all the land from the land-owners and distributed it to all the peasants who worked the land. They kicked the capitalists out. They let the people run their own piece of land for a very short time, but this was an economic disaster. Their next step was volunteer village co-operatives. The people, after much political pressure, rented their land to the co-op. They combined all the farms, consolidated them, improved irrigation, production etc. They even paid the peasant a small amount of rent for his land.

The subtle steps to complete government control continued. The peasants were eventually required to deed the land to the co-op (which was theoretically owned by the people, but completely controlled and regulated by the Communist government). This took quite a bit of political convincing but was finally accomplished. Of course, some large area farms are run and owned directly by the government. But now the peasant gets only what the co-op (government and party) decide to give him in the way of a small percentage of rice depending on his contribution in labor to the co-op farm. They did leave him a small garden plot of his own so they can say every peasant owns part of Vietnam.

The Communist Party has completely discouraged religion. They have substituted in its place patriotism and nationalism. That is the bond that holds the people together. Their moral code, according to Ho Chi Minh, is "anything that is good for, or will help our people's government — Vietnam — is morally right." That's the old Communist slogan, "Any means to accomplish an end." They have substituted the Communist Party for God.

A People's War

"The Vietnamese war is a people's war." I suppose I heard that from my interrogators a thousand times. The Vietnamese people, each individual, each family, were trained soldiers, dedicated to their cause, fighting the enemy for the survival of their country They wanted all the Vietnamese people to believe that enemy was a foreign invader (USA) and not really a communist takeover of South Vietnam.

93

Yes, it was a people's war. The North armed their people. Every man, woman, or child that could hold a gun had one. The people supported their government completely because they believed them. They didn't know any better, and never will under Communism. It was a war against an ideal, a political war.

For the people in South Vietnam, it was a war against Communism. It was not a war for conquest. It was a war against a Communist government being imposed on a people that were anti-Communist; a people who wanted freedom and democracy. This war separated families, groups, and villages in South Vietnam. Who was the enemy? People were! Groups of people, individual people, young and old, were the enemy. These people (whole villages of Viet Cong) would set traps and ambushes, be spies, conduct espionage, and kill Americans and South Vietnamese soldiers at every opportunity. They were an enemy that would not wear a uniform or fight in the daylight as soldiers. They would conceal themselves as harmless civilians and friends during the day, then become bloodthirsty fighters at night. Old men and women, young boys and girls were the enemies. In many cases it was kill them or they would kill you. Yes, it was tough to fight a war in a strange land where you could not tell friend from foe — but they knew you.

Because this enemy did not wear a uniform and would not admit being members of an organized armed force, they did not qualify as military prisoners under the terms of the Geneva Convention. They could be treated as a spy with none of the privileges of a normal POW. So their treatment, legally, could be much different. If you expected to be given the treatment of a captured military constituent, you must be wearing a uniform, insignia, and identification. Most of the Viet Cong did not qualify. Yes, it was a people's war, and each one of them was as dangerous as a professional soldier.

Chapter Ten

A POLICY CHANGE, A CHANGE OF LIFE

The first sign of any improvement in treatment was just before Christmas in 1968 when the "V" said they were going to allow us to receive packages from home. After two or three years, they were finally going to comply with one of the provisions of the Geneva Convention on treatment of prisoners.

Geneva Convention

Many Americans are not familiar with the Geneva Convention or its effect in Vietnam. The following is a very brief summary:

For over 60 years international agreements had attempted to formalize the neutral status of the POW. The Hague Convention of 1907 and the Geneva Conventions of 1929 and 1949 were the most important. Actually there were four Geneva Conventions of 1949, but the agreement of particular interest is the "Convention Relative to the Treatment of Prisoners of War."

North Vietnam acceded to the Geneva Convention in 1957 which the United States had ratified in 1955. South Vietnam agreed in 1965 to be bound by the earlier accession of Vietnam in 1953. The NFL (National Liberation Front) or Viet Cong should have been bound by either the North or South Vietnam accession.

North Vietnam had argued for years that the Convention was not applicable to any part of the conflict in Southeast Asia because war had not been declared, and the state of war had not been recognized by more than one party to the conflict.

The U.S. pointed out that Article 2 provided that "the present Convention shall apply to all cases of declared war or any other armed conflict which may arise between two or more of the High Contracting Parties, even if the state of war is not recognized by one of them."

Both the U.S. and South Vietnam and every other reasonable person in the world would agree it was certainly "armed conflict between two or more of the contracting parties." Also, the position of the ICRC (International Committee of the Red Cross) was that the Geneva Convention did apply in the Vietnam conflict.

North Vietnam also asserted that the Geneva Convention did not protect American military men who were shot down and captured in North Vietnam, because these men were not prisoners of war but were instead "air pirates" or "criminals" subject to punishment according to its laws. This refusal to afford American aircrewmen POW status was based on their reservation or exception to Article 85:

> *Prisoners of war prosecuted under the laws of the Detaining Power for acts committed prior to capture shall retain, even if convicted, the benefits of the present convention.*

North Vietnam reservation was based on their assumption that bombing North Vietnam without a declaration of war constituted a war crime, and that POWs prosecuted for and convicted of war crimes or crimes against humanity did not enjoy the benefits of Article 85.

Our government's position was that charges included in North Vietnam's reservation were not generally considered applicable to men in combat but instead to national leaders who had capacity to plan and initiate a war.

No American POW was ever prosecuted and convicted of war crimes that I know of. Did North Vietnam have the right to take reservation or exception to "any" of the provisions or articles? They refused to accord American POWs even the most basic requirements of the Convention. Here are a few of the provisions which they violated.

> 1. *Article 13. "Prisoners of war must at all times be humanely treated. Any unlawful act or omission by the Detaining Power causing death or seriously endangering the health of a prisoner of war in its custody is prohibited, and will be regarded as a serious breach of the present Convention . . . . Likewise, prisoners of war must at all times be protected, particularly against acts of violence or intimidation and against insults and public curiosity. Measures of reprisal against prisoners of war are prohibited."*

We were not humanely treated. They caused the death of several men and endangered the health of all POWs. Almost all of us were displayed, intimidated, and publicly insulted many times. Reprisal measures were also frequently used. We could almost tell how the war was going by the treatment.

2. *Article 17.* *"At the beginning of captivity, every prisoner when questioned is required to give only his name, rank, date of birth, and serial number . . . . No physical or mental torture, nor any other form of coercion, may be inflicted on prisoners of war to secure from them information of any kind whatever. Prisoners of war who refuse to answer may not be threatened, insulted, or exposed to unpleasant or disadvantageous treatment of any kind."*

Every word of that article was violated with every POW many times.

3. *Article 23.* *Directs the Detaining Power to provide information regarding the geographical location of prisoner camps to the prisoners' country.*

Of course they did not comply. They did reveal the location of a small prisoner camp right next to their one and only steel plant, in hopes we wouldn't bomb it.

4. *Article 26.* *"The basic daily food rations shall be sufficient in quantity, quality and variety to keep prisoners of war in good health and to prevent loss of weight or the development of nutritional deficiencies."*

Wow! There was no variety nor quality. We did not remain in good health, and every POW there lost considerable weight. I went from 185 pounds to about 130.

5. *Articles 34–38.* *Provide that prisoners may practice their religion, undertake intellectual and educational pursuits, and have the opportunity for physical exercise including "being out of doors."*

The "V" strongly forbid all of these pursuits, and many men spent literally months and even years in a cell with no outdoor time.

6. *Articles 39–42* *Deal with discipline in the camps and require proper respect for officers and the posting of the text of the Geneva Convention where it will be available for all prisoners of war to read in a language they can understand.*

They did not respect us as officers. In fact we had to bow to their enlisted men, civilians, and even the kitchen help. I never saw a copy of the Geneva Convention.

> 7. *Article 70. "Immediately upon capture, or not more than one week after arrival at a camp, even if it is a transit camp . . . . every prisoner of war shall be enabled to write direct to his family, on the one hand and the Central Prisoners of War Agency, on the other hand, a card similar, if possible, to the model annexed to the present Convention, informing his relatives of his capture, address, and state of health. The said cards shall be forwarded as rapidly as possible and may not be delayed in any manner."*

I have never seen such a card, and was not allowed to write for almost three years, some men for five years.

> 8. *Articles 69-77. Provide that POWs may write a minimum of two letters and four cards per month and receive frequent mail and free receipt of parcels from their families.*

Until late 1969 only 110 of the men were allowed to write at all to their families, and only 250 letters were received from 1964 through 1968. After October 1969, over 200 additional men were allowed to write and up to September 1970, over 1,200 more letters were received. If POWs had been allowed to write as provided for in the Convention about 3,000 letters and cards would have been received by their families each month.

I received about 20 letters during my six years of captivity, and my family received 20 letters from me. None of these were within the first three years, and many of these were not received until the last month. (One of the POWs found a big stack of undelivered letters in the transom over the door of one of the quiz rooms. He was able to smuggle some of them to his room and notify some of the men of the contents.) The DRV (Democratic Republic of Vietnam — North Vietnam) said families could send one parcel every two months. I received seven or eight in six years.

> 9. *Articles 77-110. Provides for immediate release of POWs who are sick or wounded and POWs long held in captivity.*

Many POWs were sick or wounded, and many died in captivity because of their injuries. Only nine men were repatriated early; eight of these were POWs less than two years. Some POWs were held almost eight years. I would call that a long time.

> 10. *Article 120. Provides for wills, death certificates, burial and cremation of POWs who died in captivity in order to ensure proper accountability and record keeping by fully identifying the dead prisoner and by recording the date, and place of burial and sufficient information to identify the graves.*

I'll bet the families of MIA/KIAs who haven't returned would like an accounting like that. North Vietnam agreed to provide an accounting for all American MIA/KIAs in Southeast Asia.

> 11. *Article 121. Requires that every death or serious injury due to an unknown cause or the act of another person shall be the subject of an official inquiry by the Detaining Power.*

Therefore, it should be a very simple matter to account for all the MIA/KIAs in North Vietnam.

> 12. *Article 126. Provides that representatives of the Protecting Power and delegates of the ICRC (International Committee of the Red Cross) shall have access to all premises occupied by POWs and shall be able to interview the prisoners without witnesses.*

North Vietnam refused this completely.

It is easily seen now that North Vietnam did not live up to the provisions of the Geneva Convention, even in a token way, as evidenced by the testimony of all the POWs.

Precious Packages

We received our first packages in February or March of 1969. My first package was quite a blessing. It didn't come in time for Christmas as promised by the Vietnamese. But when it did come, it contained some very precious articles that I was to make great use of. For instance, there was a large blue towel. In the winter I put it over the two bricks that I had on my bed for a pillow. In the summer I put it over either the bamboo mat or the blankets (which I used as a mattress in the summer) to absorb most of the sweat. And, believe me, there was a lot of sweat in the summer. There was some after-shave cream that I really needed after my weekly shave. By using the after-shave very sparingly, I made it last almost a year. But I never received any more in any other package. (They finally let us shave twice a week, but the blades were still pretty bad.) The greatest treasure of all in the first package were ten little snapshots of my family. Oh, how I treasured those. They were the only ones I was to have for a year. About six months later we received our second package, and about three months after that, our third.

In talking with my family after my return, we figured that I had received about 8 of the 20 packages that were sent to me, and approximately half of the items sent in each of the packages that I did receive. The Vietnamese kept our packages for several months, very thoroughly inspecting and mutilating them. They cut everything — even cashew nuts, peanuts, and vitamin pills — into tiny pieces. They were afraid that messages might be smuggled to us in the packages. (They were right, messages were smuggled in)!

Possible Package Items

Here is a list of the package items we valued greatly, or would have valued, if we had received them. Of course, we would not have been allowed to have many of these items, but they were sorely needed:

Medicine
Antiseptic soap
After-shave lotion
Aspirin
Throat lozenges
Foot powder
Vaseline
Powder
Pepto Bismo tablets
Anahistamine nasal spray

Clothes
Thermal underwear
Undershorts (not jockey type)
Socks
T-shirts
House–slipper socks

Miscellaneous
Close-up pictures
Professional pictures:
    A few each month
    chosen very carefully
Toothpaste
Playing cards
Checkers
Magazines

Miscellaneous
Nail clippers
Needles
Comb
Toothbrush

Books
Bible
Dictionary
History
Poetry
Atlas
Language
Math
Sports Summary

Food

Canned meat/ham	Freeze-dried dinners
Freeze-dried coffee	Freeze-dried anything
(for those who drink it)	Instant hot chocolate
Instant breakfast drink	Dried milk (dehydrated)
Cheese	Nuts in can
Peanut butter	Jam (if not in bottle)
Honey	Vitamins

Another Move

On my birthday, 29 July 1969, there was a move of POWs within the camp. I was taken to another building and put in with two other POWs: Navy Lieutenant David "Jack" Rollins and Air Force Captain Thomas S. Pyle, II. None of us were pilots.

Jack Rollins was an RIO (Radar Intercept Officer) on the U.S.S. Kitty Hawk. He was flying the back seat of a F-4B (Phantom Jet) when he was shot down over the infamous Thanh Hao Bridge. The bridge was a main link on Highway 1 from Hanoi to the south. The "V" claimed to have shot down 99 of our aircraft which were trying to knock out that bridge. Jack's mission was to knock out the surrounding flak sites with rockets. They rolled in, fired the rockets at a flak site, and then the engines stalled out. The engines wouldn't start and they were quickly at tree-top level, very close to the ground. He ejected, but there was not enough time for his parachute to open. He hit on an angle feet first in a rice paddy and sunk deep into the mud. He almost drowned and seriously injured his back (broken in two places), and perhaps sustained other internal injuries. His was quite a story; he is very lucky to be alive. There aren't very many men who can say they ejected from a high-speed jet aircraft, their parachute didn't open, and they lived to tell about it.
Jack's fine family, his wife Connie, and three children were living in San Diego.

Tom Pyle was an F-105F Wild Weasel EWO like myself. His pilot was Major Robert J. Sandvick, whom I got to know later in prison, and is a really great guy. Before coming to Vietnam, Tom had been in B-52s. He had been given an early spot promotion to captain and was an outstanding officer and good friend. Tom had gone through quite an experience as a POW. He had experienced an appendicitis attack, was finally taken to a hospital in Hanoi, had an appendectomy performed, and was back in his cell in a matter of several hours. Conditions were very unsanitary and crude. They gave him some kind of anesthetic, but they got tired of waiting for it to take effect and started the surgery anyway. He recovered all right.

Longed For Letter Finally Arrives

It was in late October, 1969 that I was allowed to write and received my first letter. Almost all the men in our camp were allowed to write and start receiving letters then. That first news from home was very welcome indeed. My first letter was from my Mom. She and Dad and the family were all fine. She seemed much improved since before I was shot down. This was great news. My sister Lorna who had multiple sclerosis was doing great. But there was not much about my family; just "Ruth and children are all fine." I received about 20 letters during the last three years; several of these were received the last few weeks.

The letters we were allowed to write and receive were on a specific format, only six short lines. My family received about twenty letters from me — about one every two months of my last three years. But even during those three years there were periods of up to one year during which they received no letters. Letters from home also had to follow the six-line format. And if they were sent through an antiwar agency, they stood a much better chance of getting to me.

You would be surprised at how many words we could get on those

Dearest Ruth, children, Family: I was not injured or wounded.
I am in very good Health so don't worry about me. I received
two packages with pictures. thanks. Send more of same - (after-shave,
Pepto-Bismol pills, Vaseline, antiseptic powder, squeeze nose drops,
Calamine lotion. How much pay do you receive and have saved?,
Health of you-all? I love, miss, want, need you, and pray etc.

NGÀY VIÊT (Dated) *11 October 1969*

Jay's first letter home

*The first "letter" after 34 months — "Jay is really alive!" say
members of his family: Mom and Dad, front row; Carla,
Larry, and Lorna, his sisters and brother, back row*

six short lines. If I printed very small, I could get almost 150 words. We would go to a quiz and in front of the interrogator write a rough draft of the letter (one per month, if we were lucky, from that time on). Of course, we had been composing it in our minds for weeks and had it memorized. Then the letters were very carefully censored by at least three different Vietnamese officers at different levels of responsibility. A week or two later we would go back and write the final approved draft, or what was left of the original draft. Anything that was of a religious nature, or a word or thought that they didn't understand, would be censored out. One POW ended up with less than one line.

When we would receive a letter we would go to a quiz, be given the letter to read for about five minutes and then never see it again. A few men got to re-read several of their letters in later years, but not many. In the last two weeks of our captivity, the "V" returned to us some (but not all), of the letters they had received earlier, but had never given us.

A Change in Their "Never Changing Policy"

It was in late 1969 that the "V" changed their policy toward us. Things improved a little. Besides being allowed to write and receive a few letters, they stopped calling us "criminals" and started calling us "prisoners." We no longer had to bow every time a Vietnamese came near us. (Previously, if we did not bow, we were beaten or severely punished.)

I believe the change was brought about by political pressure on the Vietnamese government by the U.S. government and the American people — especially, for instance, the tens of thousands of letters sent to Paris and Hanoi protesting the treatment of POWs. The concern, faith, and prayers of families, friends, and the American people also surely helped.

The "V" did something very strange to "improve" our conditions. They gave each POW an "Easter basket." Well, that's what we called them! It was a round basket about a foot high with a lid. Inside it was slightly insulated and was made for a small teapot to fit in. We were given small teapots or jugs in which to keep our drinking water. The jugs held about a pint of water. The "V" gave us water twice a day just before meals. They would bring the water to a boil over a fire, and then carry it in large kettles on choggy (carrying) poles to the POW rooms. Sometimes the girls or women from the kitchen would bring them. They were not very good looking, even after six years. They would take our little jugs, fill them and hand them back to us. The water would still be very very hot, and the jugs would be very hot. The water would stay warm for hours in the Easter baskets. In the winter it was great to have hot water to drink. (We always had cold water for bathing). The heat also delayed the growth of the water. Yes, the water would grow: you could see all kinds of bacteria and white growth in the water after it sat for just a few hours. In the summer the water in the jugs would stay hot all day long. Hot water to drink when the temperature is 100 to 120 is not very thirst quenching.

I think it was about November of 1969, while I was still with Jack and Tom, that the Vietnamese again asked us to make chess sets for the prisoners. But this time I refused, saying, "I know what you did with them last time. We had them for only a few months, and then you took them away." They promised that this time we would be allowed to keep them. Finally, after much debate, we decided to make the chess sets. Again sixty-seven cardboard chess sets were manufactured. We did, in our own way, get to give a Christmas gift to the other prisoners in our camp.

A Short Move

Before Christmas of 1969 I was moved into the next room and met my new roommate, Navy Lieutenant Lenard Eastman. "Len" was a Navy pilot, about 6 foot 2 inches tall, dark, nice looking, and a young bachelor. Len and I got along well and shared many interests, especially skiing. Len's roommate before me was Lieutenant James Joseph Connel. Both Connel and the man in the room next to Len and Connel, Captain Glenn Cobeil, disappeared from our camp the day before I moved in with Len. They were in fairly good health then, but they were not released with us. Their remains were returned in about May of 1974. We believe that Glenn Cobeil had been tortured so severely he had been driven insane and finally killed by the "V". (They couldn't return home a prisoner that was insane).

For Christmas of 1969, we were allowed to sign and send two "Christmas" cards home.

Inspiration and Strength From Poetry

While in this building we called "the barn," with Len as my roommate, something very important to our mental and spiritual health happened. We were starved for knowledge, for facts, for something to do to keep our minds active. Some of the men in the building really helped the morale of all of us. They knew a little

Spanish so they started passing Spanish vocabulary words and some grammar to us through the walls by tap code and the "cup" method. We did not have any way to write it down at the time but we tried to memorize it and pass it on, a little at a time.

This was not all however, for one of the men had been inspired by his mother when a young man to memorize poetry. What a wonderful blessing this was to us now, under these conditions. How grateful we are to him and his mother. I think the first poem that we received (a few lines a day over many weeks) was "Invictus" (see preface of book). This really inspired us and gave us courage in those trying times.

My favorite poems were "Gunga Din," "The Ballad of East and West— 1889," "The Highwayman," and "If." Two of my most admired sonnets were: "Shall I Compare Thee to a Summers Day," and "Let Me Not To the Marriage of True Minds Admit Impediments." Another poem we learned was "High Flight." This poem really lifted our spirits and morale because it said so beautifully what we had all experienced and felt so deeply in our hearts about flying. We were told the author, John Gillespie Magee, Jr., was a flying officer in the Royal Canadian Air Force, that he was killed flying, and the poem was found in his belongings. It really touched our hearts.

High Flight

Oh, I have slipped the surly bonds of earth
    And danced the skies on laughter-silvered wings:
Sunward I've climbed, and joined the tumbling mirth
    Of sun-split clouds — and done a hundred things
You have not dreamed of — wheeled and soared and swung
    High in the sunlit silence. Hov'ring there,
I've chased the shouting wind along, and flung
    My eager craft through footless halls of air.
Up, up the long, delirious, burning blue
    I've topped the windswept heights with easy grace
Where never Lark, or even Eagle flew.
    And, while with silent, lifting mind I've trod
The High untrespassed sanctity of space,
    Put out my hand, and touched the face of God.

John Gillespie Magee, Jr.

Religious scriptures, such as the Sermon on the Mount, and the Twenty-Third Psalm, were passed through camp and memorized. These were very important to me. Each Sunday I would go over all the poems, etc. I had memorized, but especially the scriptures. I would have my own little church service, reciting the scripture I could remember, singing (almost to myself) all the religious songs I could remember, and praying.

Camp Faith

On my birthday, 29 July 1970, we moved from the "Zoo" to a camp about twenty miles from Hanoi we called Camp Faith. In each compound there were about fifty men living in five or six rooms. Five or six men lived in most of the rooms, but the room I was in had thirteen — quite a change from just two or three. For the first time we were allowed to see other prisoners in the other rooms in our compound. We could even talk to them outside in the compound. There were other compounds nearby, but we had only very limited contact with them. We started receiving packages almost every two months in this new camp.

Chapter Eleven

A POW REUNION AT THE HILTON

In broad daylight in November of 1970, the whole camp was suddenly moved back to the Hanoi Hilton. In fact, it seemed that every prisoner in North Vietnam was there. Later we found out why. There had been an American military rescue attempt on Camp Hope, a short distance from Hanoi-Son Tay. (The rescue attempt would have been successful, except that the American prisoners had been moved to Camp Faith four months before.)

Now there were very crowded conditions — fifty of us in one room. In each of six or seven other rooms there were also forty to fifty men. The rooms were about sixty feet long and maybe twenty-four feet wide. That is pretty crowded for fifty men. In each room the cement bunks were either down the middle of the room (leaving an aisle around the edge) or on each side of the room. Each man got about nineteen inches wide of space (six feet long) for his bed and all his belongings. It was extremely crowded, especially when the mosquito nets with all their supporting ropes and strings were put up each night. It made quite a maze.

But having this many men in a room proved quite an advantage to us. We could get better organized. Our completely organized, military structure was so effective the Vietnamese almost gave up completely trying to get any information or propaganda from us from that time forward. We were quite a group, not the usual prisoners of war. We were not eighteen-and nineteen-year-old draftees. Our average age was thirty-five, and we were all career servicemen. Almost all were officers, very experienced and mature. Almost all had at least one college degree. Many had master's degrees. There were many men who had gone to professional military academies. We could share our knowledge and help each other a great deal.

POW College

We immediately started teaching each other college-level classes. We had five language classes: French, Russian, Spanish, German, and English. Some men took all five. (I don't see how they did it. I flunked out of Spanish three times.) There were also math classes.

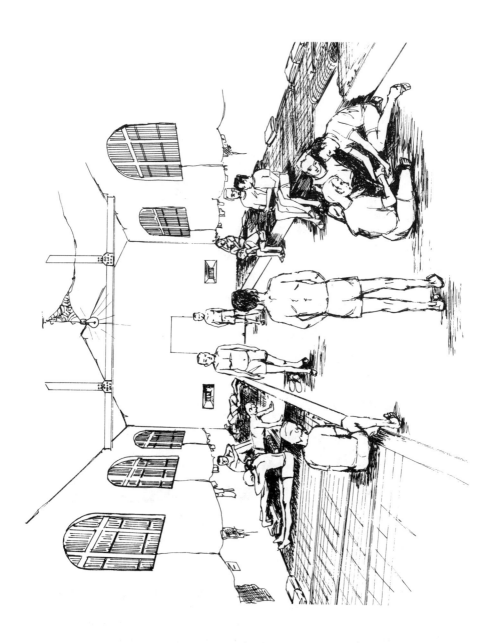

A sketch of a large room in the Hanoi Hilton

Hanoi Hilton room at night with nets up

Now bear in mind that we were teaching these classes without books, pencils, papers, or anything else from the Vietnamese. We made our own pens out of bamboo or wire. We made ink out of water, vitamin pills and medicine. The paper we used was toilet paper (a very rough scratch paper) and, sometimes, cigarette wrappers. We had to keep all of these items hidden from the enemy, because they inspected us periodically in an effort to find these things. We found if we would clean the bunks and floors a little bit that we could use them as blackboards. For chalk we had pieces of brick, pieces of tile from the roof, and different colored rocks. At first the guards tried to stop us from using pieces of tile and brick on the floor, but finally they just gave up because every time they would take them away, we would just find some more and continue to use them.

We had to decide who was going to teach the classes. With 50 men in the room, all competent in many areas, it was a difficult job. We selected as instructor for each class the man with the most expertise. He got help from other POWs and spent weeks preparing his lessons. Sometimes he worked up an outline in chalk on his bunk, and he then gave the lesson or briefing from that, using an outline, illustrations, drawings, etc.

To avoid arguments about what were facts and what weren't, we came up with the term *POW Fact*. If we said something was a *POW Fact*, then it had to be accepted as true, at least until we got back home.

The language teachers wrote a paragraph of their language down on a certain portion of the floor each day for their students to figure out. Some made it in the form of an interesting serial or soap-opera-type story. Some even combined their artistic ability, drawing cartoons with it, such as Ed Mechenbier with his German. Dave Luna taught many Spanish classes, and was very proficient. He told many movies in Spanish.

Besides languages and math courses, there were classes in history, political science, biology, astronomy, literature, and poetry. I taught classes in business, banking, accounting, family budget, speech, scouting, and religion.

We also had lectures and classes in a lighter, less academic vein: hunting and gun classes, camping, stereo, photography, and book reviews. One of the most interesting classes I taught was skiing. Just imagine fifty prisoners standing on their cement bunks practicing jump turns, stem christies, and "hot doggin it" while the Vietnamese stared through the windows and bars — wondering what in the world was going on.

Several men were gifted musically. Using ingenious methods, they taught us music history, theory, scales, chords, harmony, and so on. For example, Bill Butler used some of the men as human notes, lining them up to sing the chords and keys. Joe Crecca, who remembered a remarkable amount of classical music, would whistle all the classics and then teach us about them. To pass his course, we had to recognize and name them as he whistled them.

There were classes given by Dan Glenn, (who had been an architect) in drafting, art, and projecting house plans. Finally I got to put some of my house plans on paper and see what they really looked like. Not only that, but I was able to draw three-dimensional projections of them. We even colored them. He also drew a fabulous Paris street scene on his bunk that stayed there for many months.

We also had a very active toastmaster's club. We started out with almost everyone giving his biography. We got to know each other much better that way. Then we had rounds of all the different types of speeches: most embarrassing moment, most hilarious incident, sales talk, travelogue, persuasive speech, and so on. We also had debates and panel discussions.

POW Entertainment

There was great entertainment. We put on plays, complete with singing commercials. Sometimes we made plays of the poems we had learned. *East is East and West is West* was a hilarious production. We also put on musicals. We practiced many weeks before we put on *South Pacific* and *Sound of Music*. We did them with all the parts and costumes, and they were hilarious, too. We also told each other movies and stories. We had some skillful movie tellers in our midst. One man, Mike Brazelton, told hundreds of movies and could name the major actors and actresses in every one of them. He was a very popular roommate. Some made up their own movies. Dave Gray started telling a movie, and was told that he could continue telling the movie every night as long as it was interesting. So he started telling the movie about one or two hours each night. After twenty-seven days he was moved to another room, and his former roommates never did get to hear the last of that movie. He was still going strong. Of course, there were a few parts in it that we thought we'd heard in other movies (at least they seemed similar), but it was entertaining.

We had American playing cards for a few months, but they were taken away from us. (They took everything American away in December, 1970: toilet articles, games, and so on.) They substituted one deck of Vietnamese playing cards for each room, and once every six months or so they would throw in another deck. They also gave us one Russian-made chess set for each room. We played chess a little, and we played bridge. We had some very exciting bridge tournaments, and just about everyone in the room participated. We even gave "master" points and played duplicate bridge.

Christmas 1970

Christmas was much better with us in larger groups. We gave little personal gifts to some of our close friends. Now that we could get together, we did many things for each other.

One friend had much trouble sleeping and keeping warm because he was allergic to the blankets. Some of us got together and collected enough white handkerchiefs (received in packages from home) to make a sheet. We decorated it with some Batman wings and gave it to him as a surprise. He was really grateful. Once in a while the guards took his sheet during inspection, but somehow he managed to get it back every time.

A good friend of mine, Ben Ringsdorf, was having trouble sleeping because of the light in his eyes. So, partly as a joke, I made him an eyeshade. I drew eyes (wide open) on the white cloth and embroidered it complete with two buttons for pupils. Wearing that, he could take a nap and still look as though he were awake. He was quite amused, but he used that eyeshade all the time. It really looked strange to see those button eyes staring out when we walked by his bed.

We also decided to draw names for gifts on Christmas Eve. Actually, we were to give two gifts: One was to be a humorous item to suit the personality of the man receiving it, and the other was to be a gift costing less than $10.00 when we got home — if we remembered. We didn't know who was giving us our gift, but we did lots of guessing. And we were always getting hints as to what the gift would be. When they were actually given, it was impressive to see the work and imagination that had gone into them. Many were absolutely hilarious, often because they were so appropriate.

We had a choir and church services. I was elected the Room Chaplain for over a year. We held the church services in defiance of the Vietnamese who tried to stop them. On Christmas Eve the Vietnamese brought into the room a Bible (the first Bible we had seen) and said we could have it for forty-five minutes. For forty-five minutes many men pored over the Bible and tried to copy from it everything they could. We were copying these things on toilet paper that we had saved and using pens and ink we had made. (We kept All this material hidden from the Vietnamese for the great majority of us were not permitted to have things like that.) When it was time to go to bed, they came to get the Bible. But because we knew they would not be giving it to any other room that night, we pleaded with them to let us keep it. Finally they relented, and several of us took turns reading and copying scripture all night. We tried to copy all of the

Christmas story and the Easter story. It was very precious to us indeed. We sang Christmas carols, told Christmas stories, and had a very nice church service. We had a good choir that sang many songs. It was a very inspiring day for us. But, of course, we were very lonely and homesick.

POW Goals for the Future

During the last few years of captivity especially, we lived, planned, and hoped for the future. We ignored the present situation, filling every moment with thoughts, hopes, dreams and plans of a future life that would begin with our release from captivity. These were more than idle hopes and daydreams. These were well-thought-out plans of action, with strong convictions of our sincere desire and intention to carry them through at the first opportunity. True, in some ways these goals were idealistic, and in some cases we have found now, after being home, that there are just not enough hours in each day to accomplish all the goals, plans, and projects we had anticipated — but we have been trying! There have been very few moments of wasted time or effort or even moments of relaxation for me. I wanted to accomplish all those goals and projects yesterday — and have been impatient that I cannot do it *all* today. I have found that these are good, worthwhile goals and they have helped me to plan for the important things in life, to improve myself and progress toward a goal. I have learned that success is not a destination but a journey. It is easier to navigate life's pathway if you pre-flight certain checkpoints along the way and know what you are striving for.

Some of our projects were money-making schemes, extensive shopping lists, books to read and write, and famous dining places to try. Some were all the activities we wanted to do when we got home. Some were projects to better ourselves, in areas such as, (1) personal improvement; (2) family development; (3) religious development; (4) career development; (5) finance and personal affairs; (6) cultural and social aptitude development; and (7) physical fitness development.

Prospective Wife Analysis Chart

Another interesting project was a method for choosing a mate. After being a prisoner for five years, I was informed that my wife had divorced me. I thought about this very deeply, but after much deliberation and prayer I concluded that I could not do anything about it. It was over and I must look to the future, not the past. I knew I would

114

want to marry again. Since I was going to be choosing a wife for life, for all time and eternity, then I had better think very seriously about what kind of a woman I wanted. Over a period of a year as a POW, I devised a very detailed statistical method for choosing a mate. I came up with eighteen major attributes I felt would be desirable in my future wife. Other POWs helped me in my research with suggestions.

Some attributes contained several categories. I weighted each attribute or category as to its relative overall importance. I rated each individual category or item, usually on a scale of minus ten to a plus ten. This rating (sometimes based on a descriptive word scale) was multiplied times the weight for that attribute or category to provide a point system for evaluation and comparison. My ratings and weights are very personal and subjective. Therefore, for my purposes here, I will just briefly describe the attributes. Each man would have to derive his own rating and weighted system. The purpose of my rating chart was to evaluate these attributes so that my selection of a mate would be based, at least in part, on an intelligent evaluation of many factors and not just emotions and physical attraction. My final decision would be made only after decisive confirmation through the Lord's inspiration in answer to my prayers. (While this is personal and is referenced to me finding a wife, it would also work for a woman choosing a husband.)

1. *Love*: Love is first and foremost. Romantic love is a very strong emotional and affectionate attraction. Perhaps physical and sexual attraction is involved and complement love, but I chose to separate the two. In analyzing love between me and a prospective spouse I would ask such questions as: How much do I love her? How much does she love me? How much does she need me? How much respect do we have for each other? How considerate and thoughtful is she? How affectionate is she? How much empathy and understanding does she evidence? All of these questions I would evaluate and give a numerical rating. This rating times the weight I selected for the attribute *Love* would equal the points for this attribute.

2. *Religion:* For a devout person, religion is a major factor that contributes greatly to the success and happiness of a marriage. If marriage partners are of different faiths it can be a constant irritation or cause irreconcilable conflicts. It should be a factor considered seriously in every marriage. If the couple are of different religious backgrounds, it is certainly a strike against them to start with.

I have very strong religious convictions as a member of The Church of Jesus Christ of Latter-day Saints. Therefore, this factor was "the" most important one for me to consider, and received by far the greatest weight. It was not just a matter of whether she was a member of the Church but my rating went from high-negative points if she was not a member and had a negative attitude toward the Church, or was very active in another Church, or not likely to join mine — to high-positive points the more active and devoted she was as a member of my faith.

3. *Sex:* Sexual attraction can be a wonderful ingredient to complement love. When combined with love and under the proper conditions of marriage (for all time and eternity, not just "till death do you part," for members of my Church), it can bring indescribable joy and happiness. But it can also exist and influence our passions, desires, and actions and have nothing to do with love. If it is just a physical attraction — it is lust! If we cannot control that physical attraction, and we yield to our passions outside the bounds of matrimony, it might gratify our passions of the moment, but it will bring untold misery, unhappiness and guilt that might last forever. One of my favorite sayings is, "Don't trade a few moments of stolen bliss for an eternity of unhappiness and regret."

In many circles of society today, it is considered "old fashioned" to enter marriage as a virgin, but virtue is not old fashioned. It is an eternal principle of truth and a commandment of God. If followed, it gives the best opportunity for happiness in a marriage and gives the person possessing it greater self-esteem, a clear conscience, high honor, and justifiable pride. I believe it is certainly not necessary or advisable to have pre-marital sex; this applies to both men and women equally. Rather than assuring sexual compatibility, it more often leads to guilt ridden feelings, a failure to be compatible because of the conditions, attitudes, conscience, and moral or religious sin involved; a bad reputation, especially for the woman; and an emotional involvement that can be disastrous to emotional stability. The first aftermath of such action is loss of trust and respect for each other and the ruin of what had once been a good friendship. The man and woman who can control their emotions and passions can be trusted, respected, and will probably be faithful after marriage. But if a man or woman cannot or does not want to control passion before marriage, there is a good possibility that the marriage certificate alone will not give them the strength to suddenly be able to control their passions when other temptations come — and they will.

If two people truly and deeply love each other I think that sex will take care of itself after marriage. There are ways to judge a person's attitudes and desires about sex without pre-marital sex. I would agree that sex is a vital ingredient of marriage and an important factor. For example, if you are repulsed by the physical appearance and not attracted sexually to a person you probably would not be satisfied with her in marriage. I would want a woman to show affection toward me, but certainly not a wanton public display. I would look for a woman that was physically attractive and appealing to me, and that was attracted to me also; but that could keep control of her emotions and passions and make sure I did, too. I believe I could discern her attitude toward sex — whether after marriage she would be capable of passion and enjoyment of sex by her mental attitude and natural warmth and tenderness. I would search beyond the physical attraction and look into her heart and spirit. Like going to a movie, physical attraction is just the interesting "short subject," not the "main feature."

4. *Morality:* This is another factor that would be very important to me. My wife would have to have very high moral convictions and actions. Honesty and integrity are perhaps the most decisive values or attributes to insure a successful marriage. If you are honest with each other and will communicate with each other, there are very few problems that cannot be worked out. Honesty, integrity and being responsible — responsible for your own actions are all vital. Sexual promiscuity would lower the rating. The woman who reserved herself for her husband would rate very high on my list. I would also consider such things as drugs, drinking, and smoking. The use of these, and the extent, would be rated, from the most negative points on the heavy addict to the most positive points for the abstainer.

5. *Personality:* I would rate her personality by how congenial, happy, and friendly she was, and whether she had a good positive attitude about life and people.

6. *Physical Attributes:* I would rate her general looks, beauty, attractiveness, neatness, pride in her physical appearance, her shape (and check her mother's too, as she may look like her after a few years and babies). I would consider her general health, her physical abilities and participation in sports. I would want a woman that is active and interested in sports. Other small considerations would be her weight, and prospective future weight, her height (compared to mine), and the color of her hair, eyes, etc.

7. *Maturity:* I would consider how emotionally secure and mature she was by her expressed thoughts and her actions, especially under stress or disturbing conditions.

8. *Intelligence:* I would consider her intelligence or IQ level. I want a woman who is intelligent, who can converse with me intelligently on many subjects, who can assist me and even advise me on some matters. I do not however, want her to be considerably more

intelligent than I, or if she were, to display that attribute flauntingly.

9. *Education:* I want a woman who is well educated or trained in an occupation or profession. First, for the same reasons as to be intelligent, for education is one way to gain that intelligence and knowledge. She must also be able to apply and use that intelligence and education, especially to help in her family. I think it is important for the woman to be able, if she ever has to, to support herself and the children. She should have an occupation or talent or training that she can use to earn a living if something happens to her husband. She also needs this self-fulfillment and security. However, I strongly believe her place is in the home, especially when the children are young. This does not mean she is tied to the home, in a slave capacity, as she can still and should have her own worthwhile interests outside the home such as Church work, school, civic work or charities or any other uplifting project. A high school education is not sufficient in our modern world. A college degree or a trade or semi-professional skill is necessary to obtain a reasonably rewarding vocation.

10. *Occupation:* Her choice of an occupation tells me a lot about her ambitions, capabilities, goals, and interests. How much could her occupation or professional ability complement my profession? Would it be an asset to our children? Such occupations as secretary, teacher, nurse, or even psychologist, would be very helpful.

11. *Children:* I want children. I want to be a father — a good father. A family is very important to me, so my future wife's attitude toward children is very important. Of course there are a number of ways to have a family: raise your own children, marry someone with children (one with four teenagers like I eventually did), or adopt children. How much your wife wants a family and how well she gets along with children and can teach, manage and relate to them is very important.

12. *Age:* Age is a factor to consider, but not as important as most people think. It is the maturity age that counts — not legal age. Extremes in the ages can cause problems, both now and especially in another twenty or thirty years. One source said that the ideal age is one-half that of the husband plus seven; but I have no idea how they decided such a thing, perhaps just wishful thinking.

13. *Family:* Observing her family would tell me a great deal about what to expect our family to be. How she gets along with her family, whether they do things together, how much respect she holds for her family, their religious zeal, their history, background, education, ambition, occupation, nationality, race, and locale — would all give me insight into possible future problems or adjustments that might have to be made.

118

14. *Independence—Dominance—Cooperation:* How dependent on me is she? Does she cooperate with me and make good suggestions? This attribute may vary from one extreme of being completely dependent on me, through a happy medium, to the other undesirable extreme of being very dominant and getting angry if she does not get her own way. A happy medium would be to make suggestions, make her desires known, make good intelligent, mature recommendations, and be able in a friendly manner to discuss them. Then both of you come to a decision or compromise and accept it. In some matters, the final decision should be left to the man, as long as he respects and considers his wife's viewpoint in a fair and righteous manner. In other matters, the decision should be the wife's. This balance of power, or teamwork (co-captain) concept should be agreed upon, but flexible.

15. *Social Aptitude:* Depending on my profession, my wife's social aptitude and skill could influence my promotions and future, so this should be taken into consideration. For example, in certain key assignments in the military service such as foreign attache duty etc., a key determining factor is my wife. The Navy is, or was, considering rating an officer's wife along with his evaluation. This category would also include her level of cultural refinement.

16. *Financial Management Ability:* This is important too. How well can my prospective wife budget and manage money? How much does she know or understand about credit, interest rates, insurance, investments etc. Has she managed her own finances? Does she save regularly? According to some studies, money matters, the lack of adequate income, or being able to manage on available income, is the number one cause of divorce.

17. *Divorce Status:* If the woman I was rating had been divorced this could increase the risk of the marriage as a general rule. Therefore, negative points, increasing with each divorce, would be given. Divorce is another strike against a marriage. However, in some cases, it is recognized that the divorce was not a fault of the wife or that many lessons can be learned from an unsuccessful marriage. Each individual situation would have to be analyzed and rated separately.

18. *Skills:* This is a very general area. Each individual skill that I think is desirable would be rated taking into consideration: (1) skill level, (2) interest, and (3) potential. Each of these three areas would be rated as follows: Cannot = minus 10; won't participate, not exposed, or no interest = 0; possible potential = 5; beginner = 10; intermediate = 15; expert = 18; competes = 20; instructor = 22; and professional = 25. In some areas it might be a poor, fair, good or

excellent type of rating. They are grouped into four major categories; each item was given a weight according to how important it was to me. Each item was rated on a sliding scale from minus ten to plus twenty five. The four groups are:

Homemaking: cook, homemaker, sew, can or bottle food etc.;

General skills: good taste, style, dress, appearance, dance, music, art, etc.;

Interests: travel, hobbies, dining, TV, movies, entertainment;

Sports: various sports I enjoy that we could have a mutual interest and participate in together.

It was a very interesting and revealing experiment, while a POW, to rate my first wife, and the women I had been considering for marriage before my first marriage. When I got home and started dating I rated several women that were future possibilities. I even let several of these girlfriends rate themselves; their reaction to my rating chart was encouraging. Of course, I did not let them know how they stood in relation to anyone else. Some of the original categories have been censored or eliminated, because a POW in a cell for six years may loose his objectivity in some areas, which called for a review of the rating chart when I was actually putting it to use.

In all fairness a prospective wife should also prepare her own rating chart of a prospective husband, possibly using many of the same categories and attributes, but also some different ones and revised ratings.

Physically Fit

We tried to keep physically fit by exercising in our rooms. By now we could go out into the courtyard twice a day for fifteen or twenty minutes. In the mornings, when most of the men went out, many of us stayed in the room, running one or two miles daily in our bare feet on that cement floor. It was pretty rough on our feet. But with the running and other exercises, many of the men got into fairly good physical shape. Barry Bridger taught many of us to stand and walk on our hands. But, of course, the enemy still did not want us to actively exercise. As a matter of fact, it was not until the last month of our captivity, when everyone knew we were going home, that they finally allowed us to organize volleyball games and to play basketball and ping pong.

The Food Improves Slightly

In the large rooms in Hanoi, the food improved. Instead of rice, we now had little French loaves of bread. However, the bread had a few impurities in it, and sometimes was made with bad flour. The Vietnamese explained that the flour had to come all the way from China. Under wartime conditions it took such a long time to arrive that it wasn't very fresh, (and you know who got the worst of it). We started getting some more meat in the form of fish. It was mostly carp. Sometimes we had it fresh, sometimes dried. Sometimes we had canned fish that looked like tuna or salmon. That was pretty good.

We had to be very careful of the canned meat and fish, however. One day the fish looked pretty dark in some of the cans. That night about 15 of us got food poisoning. I was the sickest of the lot. I thought I was going to die. Late that night they took me to a hospital in Hanoi. They took a blood and stool sample and brought me back. For about a week we got some special food — a rice gruel with a little meat in it.

Much to our surprise, we sometimes got canned meat that looked like lunch meat. In the summer of 1971 they said that because we had complained about getting only two meals a day they were going to give us a third meal, breakfast. This consisted of about half a cup of milk. It was a recombined milk that really tasted pretty good. As a matter of fact, it was a lifesaver to us. That half cup of warm milk with a little sugar in it tasted great. Once in a while we would get a cookie or piece of bread or candy instead of the milk. We also started to get pumpkin soup. However, the pumpkin was prepared a little differently. They took the pumpkin out of the field (which was fertilized with human fertilizer) straight to their table and with their handy, dandy universal tool, the machete, they slammed away at the pumpkin, cutting it into very small pieces (without bothering to wash it or take out the seeds or insides). Then they just threw it into a kettle of hot water, and served it. That was probably some of the best soup we had. Once in a while we even had potatoes. Sometimes they were a little rotten, but they tasted great. I am sure we received other bits of protein, like dog meat. If times are hard they also eat monkey meat, and I am sure we had some of that. They probably eat rats, because we found one in our soup one day. For a little while the food was getting so good (according to their standards) that we thought maybe they had made a deal with the United States or Mr. Kissinger, and they were going to ransom us by the pound.

121

Spiritual Growth

The opportunity for spiritual growth was vastly improved in the large rooms. We immediately started having church services and a choir. Of course the Vietnamese objected to the church services. When we had services anyway, they put some men in solitary confinement. Likewise they objected violently to the choir. Especially when we wanted ten or twelve people in the choir. They told us we could have only two or three. We had our choir sing, and it was very inspiring. When I was chaplain for one of the rooms, we had a nondenominational church service. I thought it would be nice to have a Sunday School, too. But how do you hold a Sunday School with a dozen different denominations in the room? I decided that it would be a good idea to begin by finding out a little bit about each other's religion. So a representative of each denomination volunteered to tell about his church, and we started out. Since most of the men were Catholic, they took the first and second Sundays to tell us as much as they could remember about the Catholic Church. And then in each successive Sunday School, members of other denominations would tell about their church. It was very, very interesting. When they were all through I took my turn. For the next several Sundays I told them about Mormonism. Most found it quite interesting. I did not try to convert anyone, because as I told them, I did not have that authority or calling. I tried to tell them the history of the church and about the gospel principles. I explained some of the common misconceptions people have about the Mormon Church. I also talked to many of the men privately, answering their questions in a little more detail. (I don't believe anyone converted due to this, but perhaps I helped increase their understanding).

In one room we took turns giving the sermon every Sunday. Every man in the room (but one) stood up and gave a sermon. These were some of the most emotional and inspiring talks I have ever heard, by some men who had never been in a church before this time. I believe that almost every prisoner there became much closer to his Father in Heaven through these experiences. Certainly I know that my strength came from a great increase in my faith in and testimony of the Gospel of Jesus Christ.

I received great joy from being able to tell my fellow POWs about my church. I received word once that Dale Osborne, who was three rooms away and badly injured, wanted to know if I could send him the thirteen Articles of Faith of Mormonism. These were sent him through our "communications network," by tapping, hand signals, or the "cup" methods through many different walls and buildings — one letter at a time.

Commander Dale Osborne

Dale Osborne's story is almost unbelievable. He was from Salt Lake City, Utah. He was a Navy A4F Skyhawk pilot, and was shot down in September 1968 on an armed reconnaissance flight. He took a direct hit from anti-aircraft fire right in the cockpit. As the shell exploded, one piece of shrapnel hit Commander Osborne's chin and lodged in the roof of his mouth, knocking him unconscious. He came to in time to eject, although his right hand wouldn't work. Then he went unconscious again. His chute opened automatically. He became conscious again on the ground. His right hand was shattered at the wrist. Bones were sticking out and his hand was just barely hanging to his arm. His left arm was broken. He was bleeding at the mouth — his teeth were knocked out and some had lodged in his head — and there they stayed until he returned home. His legs were badly damaged from shrapnel. There were two large holes in the left leg, most of the calf was gone, and there was a large hole in his thigh. His body had been punctured nearly 50 times with shrapnel.

The Vietnamese scavengers stripped him of everything and left him for dead, walking slowly away. When he came to again, he saw them and yelled at them. He received a little medical care, but no pain killer.

It was a miracle he survived the exploding shell in the cockpit and a miracle he survived the pain, considering the lack of adequate medicine and treatment. He prayed a lot — someone "up there" was looking out for him. He got no water, no clothes, and finally no treatment at all. He had malaria and infection.

He awoke one day and heard them digging his grave. Later he awoke again and found himself being lowered into that grave. He started yelling. Out he came! Another time they threw him out of a truck, leaving him in a ditch to die. He woke up in the ditch. It was dark and raining. He crawled all night and made his way to a hut. One day he was taken into a room and 15 "V" officers came in and inspected him. With all his strength he made it up on one elbow, forced his eyes open and stared back at them. I guess they decided he was worth saving. Soon after that a truck took him on a horrible trip to Hanoi. He was later put into a room with another POW to take care of him — Commander Brian Woods of Lemoore, California. Brian was not a large man, only about 5'6" tall, and Osborne was a big man, 6'3" tall, about 180 pounds. But Brian Woods nursed and fed Dale, who was so helpless, and saved his life. They became great friends.

Commander Osborne received two operations and finally could walk on a crutch. But his leg never healed — it was infected continually with a green jelly-like fluid oozing out all the time. For four and one-half years his leg had an open sore about 10 inches long and 1/4 inch wide and deep. When he was released, it was still like that, but a prouder man never walked down that gangplank when he arrived home in San Diego without his crutch. He is our "hero."

A True Brother

It helped me spiritually to finally be able to talk with prisoners of my own belief. For instance, Larry Chesley and I were in the same room for about a year. Although there were forty-six other men in the room too, our religion gave Larry and me a special bond of trust and friendship. It was very gratifying to talk with someone who loved the gospel as I do. I learned a lot from Larry. We shared our deepest feelings, hopes and ambitions. We were good for each other, and I found out what it is like to have a true brother in the gospel. I became very close friends with many other POWs too. They found out very quickly my two favorite subjects were religion and Utah, and the merits of each. I greatly appreciate their friendship.

Primitive Medicine

We found that to keep in good health it was necessary to keep our clothes and our bodies as clean as possible. It seemed that the slightest cut was sure to get infected. If we had ringworm or jock itch or heat rash, the "V" soap would irritate it, so we could not use it. The few scraps of American soap, especially antiseptic soap, were priceless to us. We would use toothpaste mixed with water for a soothing form of after shave and for chapped lips.

We even got desperate in our quest of primitive medicine and ate ashes and sticks of charcoal to help with our diarrhea problems. The most severe "kill or cure" that a few of us used was the salt treatment to get rid of intestinal worms. It consisted of mixing about half a cup of salt with water and drinking it. You would get extremely sick to your stomach, and have extensive diarrhea for a day or so. But, it seemed to work. It got rid of the worms, for a while anyway. The "V" told us not to worry about the worms, ("Why everyone in Vietnam had worms. You had to have worms or your food would not digest.")

Many of us, perhaps all, were bothered with worms. I remember one morning back in the Zoo standing around outside our building. The guard had left us for a minute, and we were talking to Everett Alvarez (he was the first POW and had already been imprisoned almost 8 years). He yelled out to us, "Hey guys, I am a mother! I just gave birth to a two-foot worm. We haven't decided on a name yet." Boy, that really cracked us up. I still laugh every time I think of it.

Letter Moratorium

The letter situation (early in 1971) was getting to us. Some men were getting one or even two letters every month, but others had never received a letter. Our SRO's kept asking why some men had not ever received any mail, but the "V" said it was because no one wrote to them, or perhaps they did not have the stamps, etc. They were still censoring our letters heavily and giving us a real bad time. We were not receiving all the packages we were supposed to be receiving either, and only a small number of the items actually sent in the packages were being received. One man got a toothbrush and tooth-paste and one pair of socks — that's all.

Well, we decided maybe we could do something about it by forming some organized resistance. A letter moratorium was pro-posed. Everyone was asked to participate. We didn't propose just to refuse to write but, on the contrary, we would write the truth for a change, and at the same time air many of our gripes and complaints. Of course, we knew the "V" would not allow the letters to be mailed. In order to be effective we strongly suggested to all the POWs that we needed 100% participation. We knew it would have to last at least six months to one year. We reasoned that in addition to the side effect of airing our gripes, perhaps they would reach a higher headquarters for response, and our action might also be used as a psychological tool by our government at the Paris peace talks.

Not all of the POWs liked the idea or wanted to do it. We had quite some discussions. Remember, at this time, almost all the POWs were in the same camp. Some of the men felt it was too much to ask because of the effect it would have on our families at home. Most felt it might help, and it would be an excellent method of passive resistance against the enemy — resistance for which they really couldn't come back and punish us, at least directly. We voted on it and then left it up to the camp SROs. They decided we would do it, but there were a very few that refused and no one was ordered to participate. We started in gradually, about ten to a room, writing "honest" letters. Within three months the "V" were so irate, confused, and unhappy they wouldn't even ask us if we wanted to write. The moratorium started in about May 1971 and lasted one year. I don't suppose we will ever know if it was really successful or not. Later we found out that one whole room had continued to write.

Chapter Twelve

THE BOMBING STARTS AGAIN —
A NEW CAMP

I was at the Hanoi Hilton, living in the large rooms, for 18 months. About May 1972, the Haiphong Harbor was blockaded, and the bombing of the North resumed. They were bombing very close to Hanoi. Occasionally, during a raid, we could see our aircraft fly over. When we would hear them or hear the bombs go off, we would cheer. We knew that the only thing the communists understand is force; and that was the only way to end the war.

The "V" evacuated many civilians and their military from Hanoi. On 13 May 1972 they evacuated 209 of us to a new camp way up in the mountains, within a few miles of the Chinese border. They tried to tell us it was to save our lives from the U.S. bombing of Hanoi. We had our own ideas, however. Perhaps it was in case of an invasion. Or, if the bombing was too bad, they could move us quickly into Red China. Maybe they were just afraid their "pawns" (in a final peace negotiation) might be hurt. Or perhaps the real reason was they thought the U.S. would try a large scale POW rescue attempt when bargaining efforts failed. Whatever the reason, we were on our way.

I Hate Truck Rides

The journey from Hanoi to the camp in the mountains was by far the worst trip of my life. Any move from one camp to another was bad — rolling up your gear inside your bamboo mat or blanket, being blindfolded and roughly led to a truck, and then being tied or handcuffed to another POW and to the truck. The trip from Hanoi to the Chinese border was very hot, rough (even the back roads we took had been and were being heavily bombed), and crowded (there were 14 POWs and four guards, plus large 50 gallon cans of gas. The cans spilled a little gas, and the fumes really smelled up the truck, which was completely enclosed with a canvas cover). It was a very long ride, (it took us 28 bumpy, grueling, horrible hours). We were really crammed in like sardines, actually on top of each other, and tied or handcuffed to each other and the truck. We kept track of where we were by sneaking peeks through sections of the canvas covering on the truck. I thought for sure we would end up in China. When we finally arrived, I didn't care where it was, I just wanted out of that truck.

DOGPATCH

An aerial view of the "Dogpatch" POW camp

Our Mountain Home — Dogpatch

We were not impressed with the new mountain camp. There were 17 of us in one building. Eight were in one room, nine in the other. The rooms were separated by a long hall and two unused small rooms. The small rooms were used for punishment. I spent a few days alone in one room because of my "bad attitude" toward the guards. It was like living in a dark, damp cave or dungeon. The buildings were almost completely below ground level, like a basement house. The walls were of very thick stone and cement, the ceilings two to four feet thick. There were very small slits for windows. They put shutters on them to stop the light, and (they hoped) to prevent us from communicating between buildings. The floors were concrete and wooden planks served as beds. The cells were dark and damp all the time. For awhile our building had about a foot of water in the hall and several rooms. The rats roamed at will during the night, and sometimes in the daytime, too. There were many spiders, and we killed two very poisonous snakes at the foot of my bed. It was pitch black at night. With eight men, a small room, and mosquito nets with tie strings in every direction, getting up in the night and trying to find the little closet latrine was a maze of frightening frustration. There was no electricity in the camp. They gave us two very small kerosene lamps for four rooms. We could only burn them as low as possible for a few hours each night. Even then we would run out of fuel and spent many nights in pitch black darkness.

We had a camp-wide contest to choose a name for the mountain camp. Such names as Mountain Retreat, Mountain Home, Stone Mountain, Rock City, and Millers Cave lost to the name "Dogpatch."

Mosquito Fights

I remember well being bitten hundreds of times by the mosquitoes, especially at night. For several months I tried to get a new mosquito net. In over five years, mine had just worn out and was coming apart. It had many holes in it, especially along the seams. I tried to patch it, but it didn't help much. It was too hot to sleep with anything on but your shorts. It was quite a battle between the mosquitoes and me. It was pitch black, and I could not see them. So I would lie very still and feel them alight on me; then very slowly and quietly get my hand in position — and wham! I'd slap them. I didn't count it a "kill" unless I could squish it in my fingers after the hit. It was not uncommon to be a triple ace or to make twenty to twenty-five kills a night. My best effort was 49 one night. I finally got a new net.

Communication Still Vital

We set up another camp-wide communication system, but it took many weeks and ingenious methods to get it established. Each building had a small enclosed patio with solid rock walls and a covered roof. We never got outside this area until the last month or so. This enclosed outside room had two cement sinks which were filled by a bamboo pipe system on an irregular basis when it rained. We did the dishes and bathed in this area. The buildings were all about 30 yards apart and set at odd angles so we couldn't see directly into another building's windows. The walls were so thick that we could not tap from one room to another, let alone from one building to another.

The "V" were getting smarter in trying to prevent communication between buildings. We used hand signals where we could, or flash a card in front of a crack in the door sending Morse code, or flash a white plate in a window.

Food and Activities

We went on a diet of rice, terrible-tasting-combination-of-anything soup and, occasionally, water buffalo meat. We called it "bafah-blow." It was very tough, stringy, and mostly gristle, but sometimes it tasted pretty good. We received two or maybe three food packages from home in the nine months at this camp. They must have kept most of the goodies because these were much smaller than others we had received in the past. When we got our packages from home, we were sometimes allowed to build a fire out in our patio wash area to warm up water for coffee, soups, or hot chocolate mix, etc. We took turns cutting wood (with a machete), building, and tending the fire. It was here I put to good use some of my Boy Scout skills. We only got two matches, no paper, and usually wet wood. We were allowed to write a letter each month, but we found out later (as we suspected) none ever reached home. The letters we received were few and far between; I received four in that time.

Roommates

We kept up our classes (mostly languages and math), toastmaster's club, church services, choir, movie telling, etc. I am particularly indebted to Dave Carey. Dave was a very good natured Navy flier, who had a winning smile and fiery red hair. Slowly and diligently, day after day for many months, he tried his best to teach me Spanish. This makes him the most patient man in the world. "Muchas gracias, amigo mio."

Another friend and roommate (we called each other roommates instead of cellmates) was Lieutenant Al Brudno. Al was probably the most intelligent POW I knew. He was an MIT graduate and an outstanding young Air Force officer. His great ambition was to be an astronaut, and he might have made it. Al was very knowledgeable and talented, but very quiet. He kept to himself most of the time. He taught some classes in higher math and physics, doing problems like space shots, join-ups in space, etc. He had a remarkable memory and drew (from memory) quite a detailed map of the world, especially of Africa. He could name every country in Africa and most of the capitals. It was very accurate. Then he gave some very interesting lectures on all the countries.

Al was very devoted to his young wife. They had not been married very long. Much earlier, during some of the worst years for POWs, Al decided to compose an epic poem to her. At the time he knew nothing about poetry, and he had never done much creative writing. But Al was a perfectionist. A POW in the room next to him was an English major in college. Every day he would teach Al all he knew about poetry, which was considerable. When Al had all the basics down pat, he began. It became a complete obsession with him, but a wonderful obsession. He was so completely absorbed in his mental ordeal that sometimes he would not eat, sleep, or talk to his several roommates for days. He, like most of us, had no pencils, notebooks, or paper. He was composing this poem mentally. As I recall, it took him about four months to complete and was 127 verses of eight lines each (without one word written down). Every word had to be the perfect one for description, rhyme, meter, etc. Sometimes he would go for days trying to decide the exact one word to use. With his strong math and scientific background, it had to be mathematically perfect also.

When it was all finally completed it was still a mystery because, to Al, it was personal, it was private, it was Al. It wasn't until several years later, one night in Dogpatch, that we finally talked Al into reciting his epic poem. It was truly a masterpiece. It was a very moving, personal, perceptive, and emotional story. Parts of it were personal, best left (after our moment of appreciation) just for Al and his wife — unpublished. Some of the descriptive passages about captivity and our conditions, however, vividly described our inner-most thoughts and feelings that we had been incapable of transferring into our own words. Al contributed much to satisfying the mental appetites of his fellow POWs. He was also one of the lead men in the infamous Hanoi March of 6 July 1966, where he and all the other POWs in the march took much physical abuse at the hands of the stirred up mob of Vietnamese people.

Major "Mo" Baker was a building SRO (Senior Ranking Officer). I have never known a finer officer and friend. He was so well liked and respected that I am sure he would have won a poll for the most popular POW. He was almost like a father or big brother to us. He taught many math classes, gave us advice when we asked, and held us together as a team.

Mike Brazelton announced one day he had another movie to tell us, a long one. We always enjoyed listening to Mike's many movies. I don't know how he could remember so many details of so many movies. Well, Mike took two nights to tell this particular movie. We were really impressed and spellbound. It was a World War II story about American fighter pilots in England, plus a corollary showing the German side of the war, complete with love affairs and everything. We were going to vote it an "Emmy" for the outstanding movie told. But it was strange that such an outstanding, interesting move had not been seen by anyone except Mike. Then he admitted that it wasn't a movie or a book; he had made it up himself.

Captain Charles Green was another very likeable and extremely good-natured roommate who, I hope, is still a good friend. You see, Charlie was one of the few men I could talk into being my partner for an occasional bridge game. My system was not exactly according to "Goren," but we had some interesting and fun games. Perhaps they were a little exasperating to Charlie, but he was a really good sport. Charlie and I enjoyed talking about sports such as hunting and fishing. I made him brief me several times on all the details he knew about his parents' safari to Africa. Charlie and I had both been Eagle Scouts and really think a lot of the program. We, along with two other friends, Bob Jeffrey and Tom Storey, gave about a four night series of lectures on the Boy Scout programs. This was in a large room at the Hanoi Hilton. In this same room we once talked Charlie into dressing up in a hilarious outfit like "Pogo" in the funny papers. It was for a special skit we had. He had on an outlandish green outfit complete with a long curling tail. He made the outfit up from bright green American towels and shirts received in some of our packages. He really gave us a good laugh, and we greatly appreciated his humor.

Mike Christian was determined to learn to play the guitar, and so he made one. Well, at least, he made something he could practice on. He found a long, narrow piece of wood and attached some strings made of braided thread. It worked well for strumming and fingering techniques — except that it produced no sound. Mike made up for that with his singing.

Another interesting and likeable roommate was Lieutenant Richard Brenneman. Everyone liked Dick, just like you would love your favorite old dog. As a matter of fact, "Dog" was his nickname. It was with respect that we called him "Dog," and he actually insisted we call him that. However, very soon we called him "King Dog" because of his royal plans. He had more projects for making money than anyone I had known, and he did things up big — royally." He designed the largest tract of mobile home parks in the USA and the largest mushroom-shaped space-capsule-type home imaginable. He really was very talented and creative. He designed his own airplanes, boats, and sports cars. It wouldn't surprise me at all to find out he had built them all. "Dog" was not married at the time he was shot down, and he wanted to remain single his entire life. He was very "dogmatic" about it! Every penny he had earned over the years went into Armed Services Overseas Savings Plan at 10% interest. So he would have a nest egg to start with when he got back. We always told him that within two years after he got home he would either be a millionaire or flat broke. "Dog" and I used to play chess and gin rummy. I usually won at gin rummy, but wow, did he get even at chess!

Little Things Meant a Lot

At this time the "V" still had not given us any books, note-books, pencils, or reading material (except their one and only newspaper, the Official Vietnamese Government *Courier*. What a one-sided piece of propaganda garbage sheet that was! Occasionally, however, we could get some news out of it by reading between the lines.) We did manage to smuggle many old notes with us, and we kept these hidden from the "V". It was extremely difficult to study or even read them because most of the rooms were so dark all the time. The guards would roam the buildings for business or inspection most anytime during the day except an hour or so at noon — siesta time. This was the best time to get the notes out and study or communicate. You could see fairly well for about an hour after we were locked up at night also. By locked up, I mean we did not have the run of the building, but were locked into the two rooms at opposite ends of the building.

I have often been asked what modern conveniences I missed most while a prisoner. If I were to be perfectly honest, I would have to say a soft bed, a hot shower, and a toilet seat. Of course, there were other conveniences we missed; the little things we take for granted all the time, such as a pencil and piece of paper, pillow, needle, knife, finger nail clipper, after-shave, hot water to shave and wash with, cold water to drink, and books.

Quite often we asked each other, "If you could receive five books, what would they be?" Some of the men chose a Sears catalog, *Playboy* magazine, and language and math books. Just about everyone, including myself, chose the *Bible* as his first book. My second choice was the "Triple Combination" (Mormon scripture containing the *Book of Mormon, Doctrine and Covenants*, and *Pearl of Great Price* all in one). Third, was a dictionary; fourth, a book with famous poems and short stories; and lastly, either a combination history/atlas or H.G. Wells's *Outline of History*. What a wealth of knowledge we could

133

have gained with a set of encyclopedias, for instance. We were indeed searching for knowledge, to keep our minds occupied.

In late fall, 1972, the camp authorities told us that progress was being made for the first time in the Paris talks between the US and North Vietnam. They even suggested a likely cease-fire in the South and that we might be going home by Christmas. They gave us some news about the talks, but it was always very one-sided and not quoting anything specific that the U.S. had offered. It was meant to discourage us. It did, especially on Halloween, when they told us the talks had broken down. But we knew it was just a matter of time.

The talks resumed again, and the "V" also knew that in a short time we would be going home. In late October, they started to give us a few more things. They gave us a pen, a very small ration of ink, and two small copy notebooks for each building. This was the first time that writing material had been given out on a general basis in all the years of our captivity. A few weeks later there was a big move within the camp. Many of us were switched around and, it seemed, grouped more or less according to approximate shoot-down date.

After another few weeks, many changes took place. We were given a few sports and science magazines that had been sent to us years before but never given to us, plus some stateside communist newspapers and anti-war articles. We saw a couple of anti-war movies and one on a circus. We were allowed to mix outdoors a little with the men in the next building for the first time. We even were allowed to clear an area outside the building in order to set up a ping pong table. Occasionally, when they would give us a ping pong ball, we could play for an hour or so. We were allowed outside the building (in the immediate area) an hour in the morning and afternoon. We were even allowed to go a short distance up to the kitchen and help prepare some of the food and carry it back to our building.

Going Home?

Things were looking up. We knew now that President Nixon would not stop the bombing until an agreement had been reached in Paris. We also knew we would not go back to Hanoi until the bombing had ceased.

After six years it wasn't so much a matter of "when" we were going home. (After that long, it seemed we could last another six, seven, or even more years, if necessary.) The question was, "How are we going home?" We wondered if we would go home with honor or if the whole struggle would have been in vain. If we went home, as some politicians recommended, as barter items ("If you withdraw your troops and all support from South Vietnam, then we will release the prisoners"), it would all have been in vain. We did not want to be released until the North Vietnamese had been defeated, until South Vietnam had a viable government, supported by the majority of its people, until South Vietnam's army could defend themselves from North Vietnam, until the country could maintain its own government. Perhaps it would not be a truly democratic government, but one with the possibility of becoming democratic over the years — certainly not a Communistic government. Once a government is Communistic, chances are it will remain that way forever. We were not bartered! We came home with honor! For that I am very thankful, especially to President Nixon, but also to the American people that supported him.

It was a very hopeful Christmas and New Years that we spent in that extremely cold mountain camp. On 20 January 1973, we took that horrible truck ride through the mountains back to Hanoi. It was just as dreadful an experience as the trip from Hanoi, 24 men to a truck, but this time we didn't really mind. We knew this would be the last trip — the going-home trip.

Chapter Thirteen

A Test of Faith

For me — and, I am sure, for most others — life as a prisoner was very difficult and hard. It was a real test of faith. For me there were many "personal" trials and tribulations. But, *I never lost faith!*

When I left home my mother was seriously ill with Alzheimer's syndrome. She had been given five years to live, and that five years had expired when I was shot down. Each day I wondered if my mother was still alive. How had she taken the shock of my being shot down? Had she given up hope over these long years? My sister Lorna also had a terminal disease, multiple sclerosis. My brother had recently been divorced. My younger sister had been divorced. And what of my own family: my wife, my three children? How were they getting along? Was my wife waiting for me, or had she given up hope? For almost three years I worried about these things. Then I received some news. First from my mother and sister: mom was all right. In fact, she was better than when I had been shot down, even though she had contracted a second terminal disease, leukemia. My sister Lorna was getting along fine with her disease, and my children and wife were okay. But time went on, and on, and still no letter came from my wife or children. Finally, after five years, I found out that my wife had divorced me and immediately married again. This hit me hard! But I did much praying about it. I tried to understand. Next I learned that my eldest daughter, Carrie (who was now 17 years old) had married, and I was going to become a grandfather! I really had mixed emotions about this. I wanted to have grandchildren, but worried that Carrie was too young.

These trials and tribulations were a real test of my faith. My mother had taught me, "Son, everything happens for the best, if you will live in tune with the Lord. Even though you don't realize it at the time, it will be for your best." I tried very hard to remember and apply those words of wisdom.

Chapter Fourteen

THE RELUCTANT "KISSINGER 20"

When we arrived back in Hanoi, via the terrible truck ride, we noticed that the precision bombing by the B-52s had done extensive damage to military targets around Hanoi. Back in the Hanoi Hilton we were put into the big rooms again. In the weeks following, we were allowed to cook our own food, had ample outside time, and played volleyball and ping pong. On 30 January 1973, the peace agreements were read over the camp loudspeakers, and a copy was given to us. The sick and injured were to go home first. Then all others, in order of shoot-down; that way, those captured first would go home first. This would occur in groups of about one hundred, (in about two-week increments, we figured). On 12 February 1973, the first 112 POWs were released. I was to be in the next group, two weeks later.

However, there were rumors of an earlier release, and then the names of 20 were sent through the walls. Surprisingly, my name was among them. We were told by our leaders to get ready to go. A few hours later, the "V" came and moved us to a different part of the camp. The next day we were told that, as a special tribute to Dr. Kissinger, 20 extra prisoners would be released early. Suspicious, we asked. "Why us? Why not the top 20 on the list according to shoot-down date?" They said they really didn't know, but that the U.S. Government had requested us by name. Then they issued us our special "go-home" clothes.

We tried to think why the U.S. would request us by name. We thought of all kinds of family emergencies: sickness, deaths, and so forth. Unconvinced, we told the "V" that we didn't believe that the US had requested us by name, and we demanded proof. Finally they admitted that the U.S. had not requested us by name, just 20 men. This really made us mad. We told them that they were just playing games, trying to make us look bad, and that they were violating the peace agreements. We flatly refused to go home this way. We told them we would wait our turn. Well, this upset the "V"; this was very embarrassing to them.

The next day our captors insisted we go, that arrangements had already been made with the U.S., and that our names had been released to our families and the press. We said, "That's tough, we are not going.

POWs awaiting release

You will have to drag us out of here."

The next day we were moved back with the rest of the POWs in a building next to them. We told our commander the story and said that we would not go unless we received his "direct order" to do so. There was much consultation. High-ranking "V" officers talked to us to no avail. Finally, high ranking military officers from the United States POW negotiating team actually came to our prison room and told us that the return of the rest of the POWs would be delayed if we did not go. So, our POW commander gave us a direct order to go. We obeyed. We were released on 18 February 1973. It was exactly six years to the day for me; actually to the hour — 0930. That is the story of the reluctant "Kissinger 20."

Guards outside the
prison rooms at Hanoi Hilton

"Kissinger 20" leaves Hanoi

(Left file, front–rear): Lt. Comdr. Fred Purrington, Capt. Joseph Crecca, Jr., Capt. Michael C. Lane, Major James R. Berger, Major Jay R. Jensen, Capt. Henry P. Fowler; (Right file, front-rear, faces showing): Capt. John H. (Spike) Nasmyth, Jr., Capt. H. (Ben) Ringsdorf, Capt. John Davies; (Door of bus): Capt. James R. Shively.

Chapter Fifteen

RESURRECTION DAY

Welcome Home

When we boarded the C-141 and took off from Gia Lam Airport, our cheers lifted that plane to freedom. That wonderful, happy feeling, as tears of joy ran down my cheeks, I shall never forget. And what a tremendous homecoming it was, landing at Clark Air Force Base in the Philippines and seeing thousands of people waiting to greet us! Bands, banners, military, old people, young people, kids — they were all there! Walking down the gangplank from that C-141 onto a red carpet amid all the searchlights, cheers, and joy was one of the happiest and proudest moments of my life. To put my feet on American soil (at least an American air base) and to see so many friendly, cheering faces was a feeling so great it's difficult to describe — you just had to be there and actually experience it.

Welcoming crowd at Clark AFB

We boarded buses to take us to the hospital. One anxious, young, teen-age girl eluded the police, ran up, and through the bus window handed me — yes — a Sears' Catalog. I waved and threw her a big kiss. She had heard for so long that POWs had wanted a Sears' Catalog. Crowds of people lined the roads all the way to the hospital, and cheered us as we passed.

The hospital rooms looked great to us, so clean and white. And all the halls in the hospital were decorated with hundreds of "Welcome Home POWs" posters made by all the young school kids. Everyone there was just great. The first thing we did was to get out of our special,

Welcoming posters on hospital walls

one-time wear, go-home Vietnamese clothes. And then we had something we had really missed — a hot shower, and then a great meal of our choice — steak and eggs.

The military briefed us on what to expect the next few days. (I found out that I had been promoted to Major in 1967.) Each of us were assigned an escort officer, a man as close to our rank, age, job, religion, etc., as they could find at Clark Air Force Base. My escort officer was Captain Duane A. Holm. He stayed with me constantly during the daytime the few days we spent at Clark Air Force Base, and even traveled to the States with me until I got to a final hospital. Duane was a great guy and really helped me out a lot. He brought me up-to-date on just about everything, answering my hundreds of questions, running errands for me, and introducing me to our local church leader there, Colonel George C. Kiser. Colonel Kiser and I had several long and pleasant talks and, since he was the chief dentist there, he even did some much needed work on my teeth. He was especially concerned about how I had taken the news of my divorce, and he helped me a great deal with my personal problems. While most of the POWs were going home to the waiting arms of their wives, I would not taste of this joy. I tried very hard not to be bitter, not to feel sorry for myself, to understand the other side. I think I do now. I am not bitter. I bear no grudge. I decided to look to the future and bury the past; to try to learn from its mistakes, but not worry or fret over things past, or things over which I have no control. The following poem means much more to me now:

God, grant me the serenity to accept the things I cannot change,
Courage to change the things I can,
And Wisdom to know the difference.

The next 48 hours were pretty hectic compared with our usual life of the past six years. As soon as possible we scheduled telephone calls to our families in the States. I talked to mine for about 15 minutes. What a wonderful heart-warming feeling to hear the voices of your loved ones after so many years.

We experienced many medical tests and an extensive physical examination. I was very happy when the flight surgeon reported that I was in excellent condition, that he could even clear me right then to fly as an aircrew-member again.

I was so impressed with the welcome we had received, especially from the young students, that some of us volunteered to go over to a local grade school and give a little talk to the kids. They were really excited and interested and gave us a great welcome. We were very proud to talk to them. Little did I know then that was to be the first of over six hundred speeches that I have given to date (1989).

On To America the Beautiful

Time passed quickly. After only a few days at Clark AFB we boarded another C-141 and took off for the good, old United States of America. We stopped briefly in Honolulu, Hawaii, were given a tremendous welcome again, and had beautiful "Hawaiian leis" put around our necks. After only about an hour on the ground in Hawaii, we found ourselves airborne again, going home, where we would be sent to various hospitals around the country.

As the coastline came into view, we could see a very beautiful sight — the Golden Gate Bridge. We all started cheering, crying, and broke into song — "California Here I Come." We talked the pilot into making a low pass over the Golden Gate (with permission of course). That was a great feeling. You just can't imagine the love, appreciation, and emotion we felt for our country.

We landed briefly at Travis Air Force Base, California. There was quite a crowd to greet us. Some of the men stayed there, and some of us changed aircraft to go to our assigned hospitals. I was scheduled to go to the March Air Force Base Hospital at Riverside, California.

We took off from Travis. Three of us were going to March AFB.

Same "Kissinger 20" in Hawaii Enroute Home

Front row: Capt. John Davies, Capt. Michael C. Lane, Major James R. Berger. Second Row: Capt. Ben Ringsdorf, Capt. Henry P. Fowler, Cmdr. James G. Pirie, Lt. Comdr. Fred R. Purrington, Capt. John (Spike) Nasmyth, Jr., Major Donald L. Heiliger, Major Joseph S. Abbott. Third Row: Capt. Edward J. Mechenbier, Capt. James R. Shively, Major Jay R. Jensen, Capt. John W. Clark, Major Hubert K. (Bud) Flesher, Capt. Joseph E. Milligan. Others of the "20" who eluded the photographers: Lt. James Bailey, Capt. Joseph Crecca, Jr., Capt. Kevin J. McMannus, Lt. Comdr. Joseph C. Plumb.

It was dark on the evening of 20 February 1973 when our plane landed. Before we got out of the aircraft, we were briefed, and I was asked to say a few words to the hundreds of people, including my family, waiting to greet us. I said I would try.

I got off the plane and walked over to a microphone. I thanked all of the people for the tremendous welcome, told them we were very proud of our country, and how happy we were to be home. But then, I caught sight of my parents, family, my children, and Heidi, my granddaughter! It was too much for me! I couldn't say anymore. I dropped the mike, ran over to my family, and embraced them joyfully. What a wonderful feeling. I gave mom a big hug and kiss and took the beautiful lei that was still around my neck and put it around her neck.

Jay is greeted by mother and father
upon his arrival at March AFB

145

As I hugged my children, I couldn't believe how grown up they were. Roger was a good-looking young man; Sherrie, a real beauty; and Carrie, a beautiful young woman with a nice, pleasant, tall, handsome husband and my darling little granddaughter, Heidi. Dad looked great, and was so proud and happy.

Jay arriving at March AFB

My sister Lorna looked as pretty as ever. Her husband A.J. had not changed a bit—he was just as happy and friendly as ever. My younger sister Carla was doing fine and looked happy. My younger brother Larry had matured and was obviously delighted with his new family. It was a wonderful reunion.

Within a few minutes we were all gathered in my hospital room. It was quite an emotional scene. We were all trying to talk at once, asking a hundred questions, or else we were so choked up with happiness and tears we couldn't speak. I realized just how much they loved me and had missed me, and vice versa.

Everyone gave me the POW/MIA bracelet with my name on it that they had been wearing for so long.

Mom looked so well that I could hardly believe it. (She had been almost bedridden with Alzheimer's when I was shot down, and later also contracted leukemia). But Mom had never given up hope for one moment. From the first word of my shoot-down she had possessed undying faith that I was alive and would come home okay. She decided that if she was ever going to see me again, that she would have to get well. To the great surprise of her doctors and family, she did get better and better! Her remarkable faith was rewarded with her better health and, eventually, with my return. She now looked great and was sharp and alert — better, in fact, than she had been in ten years. She could now take care of her home, and she had traveled with Dad to Washington, D.C. and elsewhere on my behalf. She never gave up hope. She had such great faith — in God, and in me. What a test of faith, not only for Mom, but for Dad, my children, and all my family, relatives, and friends!

When the noise had subsided a little, Dad said, "Son, welcome home. A job well done. We're all proud of you." That touched me very deeply and made what I had been through seem worthwhile. All the blood, sweat, and tears were worth it. And it helped me imagine how wonderful it will be, if, when I return to my Father in Heaven, I can hear Him say, "Welcome home, son. Well done. I am proud of you." How much joy that reunion will bring!

"Never Forgotten"
Jay with two of his children

147

I was able to talk with my family and the children about the problems, the changes, and see what adjustments had been necessary while I was away. The more I found out the more I understood that Mom was right. Everything had worked out for the best, and would in the future. I was a changed man too, stronger willed, determined, dedicated, more appreciative, and much more humble. I knew that only by keeping in tune with the Lord would I be really happy. Yes, I had been in hell for six years but I felt I had just been resurrected. The day of my return, 18 February 1973, was the first day of my new life.

Over the next few days I visited with my family. We had a lot of fun at Disneyland. The children really enjoyed themselves. One of the poignant reminders of just how homesick I had been for my country and how much I loved it, was during this emotionally moving visit to Disneyland. Most memorable was the sensation of freedom and the joy that came over me and the children in AT&T's Circlevision Theater as beautiful scenes of our wonderful country unfolded on the screen surrounding us. It brought great feelings of pride in my heart, feelings that I have tried to express in a letter of appreciation:

That's what it's all about, my children — America the Beautiful! Real freedom, democracy, and happiness! As I stood so tall, so proudly singing "America the Beautiful" in Disneyland's AT&T Circlevision 360-Degree Theater, holding my tearful daughter, Sherrie, and with my hand on my son Roger's strong little shoulder. Through my own tears of joy, the full impact of what America and freedom mean, to me, and to "us" was culminated. An emotional moment we shall never forget. It symbolized so strongly what I, and millions like me, were fighting and dying for. What so many fellow Americans have died for in Vietnam.

Yes, Disneyland itself, but especially "America the Beautiful" Circlevision assured me that it was all worth it. All the suffering, strife, and deprivation, the worry and grief of my family. Six years, yes, six years to the day, of my life — and my former wife, my three lovely children — all this I gave up forever. And many others like me have done much the same, and more. For what? For America, democracy, freedom, and our way of life. So that other people, all over the world, might enjoy the same freedoms.

Yes, it was worth it — well worth the sacrifice. All our prayers have finally been answered. So, thanks, dear God, thanks Disneyland, thanks American people, and America the

Beautiful. And thanks, AT&T, for showing me and my children so vividly why I had to serve so proudly in Vietnam. That's what it's all about, Carrie, Sherrie, and Roger. That's America the Beautiful!

Chapter Sixteen

A Nation Concerned

Families Concerned

After talking with my family, I realized just how much they had missed me, worried and thought about me, prayed for me, and how much work they had done in my behalf. Dad, especially, had worked very hard for my return. He wrote hundreds of letters in my behalf, and was very active in VIVA (Voices in Vital America), National League of Families of POW/MIAs, and other organizations who were so actively trying to get us home. We owe much to these organizations. He became so engrossed in this work that he retired from his Rural Mail Carrier's job to give it his full time and effort. He and Mom

Jay's dad showing Jay the many letters

traveled extensively in this work. Dad very enthusiastically pushed the drive in October 1969 to write tens of thousands of protest letters to Hanoi via Paris. He talked many times at schools, etc., encouraging Americans to support our POW/MIAs. He answered hundreds of letters from concerned, wonderful Americans who bought bracelets to wear until "their" POW/MIA came home.

My sister Lorna wrote and answered many letters in my behalf. She was active in VIVA, sold POW bracelets, and with her husband traveled to Washington, D.C., and participated in other projects as well. One such project Lorna and family spearheaded was the Pony Express Ride for POWs campaign. Pony Express riders rode from St. Joseph, Missouri, through Salt Lake City, Utah, to San Diego, California, collecting over 60,000 letters from concerned students at local high schools urging Congress to push for the release of all prisoners, and a complete accounting of all MIAs.

Ride for POWs campaign

My sister Carla and brother Larry, also very concerned, were busy doing their part.

All the families of the POWs and MIAs were deeply and emotionally tied to news of their loved ones. This concern is apparent in the following poem my father wrote:

When the Men Come Home

This day belongs to JAY and DAVE and DON
And to all the other boys who have —

> *so long — been gone.*

We still may need to pray for their return
And scan each list of names

> *for those we yearn.*

But for these men who bear our names,
May GOD bring THEM back . . .

> *not just remains.*

This day belongs to RICK and FRANK and JOHN
And to all the other boys who have —

> *so long — been gone.*

Will they be reading as they travel home,
Of trips to the Moon, ecology,

> *and Astrodomes?*

Or will they be in silence evermore?
Oh GOD, be kind, return them as

> *they were before.*

This day belongs to JAY and BOB and BILL
As this war ends, we all can say we've

> *had our fill*

The waiting and the anguish now will end
In one way or the other,

> *let's not pretend*

Oh GOD, prepare us for our test.
When they come back, let's meet them

> *with our best.*

-Milton L. Jensen

MAJ. JAY R. JENSEN
2-18-67

JAY

IS COMING

HOME!

DEAR FRIENDS:

If it sounds like we're shouting the news, you better believe it, as we are just that anxious for you to share it with us! It is wonderful to hear that PEACE has finally arrived; that our POWs are being returned to their loved ones; that no more boys will be sent to Vietnam.

We believe that an aroused public has been the most instrumental factor in pressuring for a negotiated agreement. Thus, it has been directly through your help that we have achieved this victory of PEACE . . . . Because it has meant so much to us, both what you have done, and the moral support you have given us, we take this opportunity to thank you all.

We thank our friends, relatives, neighbors, and all who have prayed with us and for us; the Schools and Churches; letter writers and bracelet wearers; all news media; public officials throughout America and locally, a special thanks to Salt Lake City Mayor Jake Garn and Utah Governor Calvin L. Rampton.

You have all done a wonderful job, Jay, and all other POW and former MIAs are forever grateful. When in the final accounting, our hearts are saddened once more by the realization that some of the boys we prayed for and hoped for, sacrificed their lives for their COUNTRY, let us, forever, HONOR that sacrifice by never again permitting nation-wide apathy towards foreign involvements.

May the tens of thousands of POW bracelet wearers in America proudly "retire" their bracelet to the "Trophy Case," where it may become a permanent reminder of their "CONCERN."

Each list of returnees will be eagerly scanned for the names of those we have prayed for. We are literally standing on the front steps awaiting our son's return. Wish it was possible for you all to join us. Hope this letter can at least help you catch the spirit of the occasion.

THANKFUL and HAPPY,

Mr. & Mrs. Milton L. Jensen
389 West Main
Sandy, Utah 84070

Circular sent out to bracelet holders, January 1973

153

Here is another poem by Debbie Wood, daughter of Don Wood, MIA (whose remains were finally returned many years after our release), written while she was a Provo, Utah, junior high school student.

Please - Bring Him Home

I don't know what he suffers there,
I cannot feel his grief, despair —
His agony is only known
To men who have been caged—alone.

I only feel a selfish pain,
A fear that I might pray in vain
And never see again his face
Or feel again his strong embrace.

I need his love while I am young
With many fears to walk among.
I need his help to guide me through-
To him, the dangers are not new.

For how long must I wonder when
My father will be home again?
How many years can he survive?
Is he, even now, alive?

Before it is too late to try,
Before my life must pass him by,
Please, bring him home, and I'll be then
My father's little girl again.

We found out everything that had been going on in our behalf. We learned of the tens of thousands of letters sent to Hanoi and Paris by aroused citizens. Thousands of bracelets with our names on them had been worn by so many devoted, concerned Americans. Why, there were thousands that wore bracelets with my name on them, many writing me how they had prayed for my safe return, and how happy they were I was home. We found out the American people had not forgotten us. We found out about all the petitions and the political rallies for us, about the bumper stickers, pens, stamps, letter labels; and about all the other things that had been done to keep the prisoner issue alive to the American people. We found out that while in POW status, our dependents were allowed the school benefits of the G.I. Bill, and the National League of Families was pushing hard for a national POW/MIA scholarship program for our dependents to apply for after our return. Over half the States had provided this plan as of the end of 1972. Some private schools have granted scholarships, too. This would be a great benefit. No, we were not forgotten.

Believing Bracelet Bearers

I was deeply touched by the simple gratitude of all of the hundreds of Americans that wrote to tell me that they had worn my bracelet. Wearing that bracelet meant a great deal to them, and it proved to me that they "really cared," and they truly were the "standard bearers" keeping the POW issue alive.

I am taking the liberty of sharing a few excerpts from several of those letters:

Dear Major Jensen:

I am writing this letter for my young son John, who has worn your POW bracelet for several months. He wanted me to express our family's joy on your release and return home to your family . . .

John was critically hurt recently and had to undergo a series of operations, but he refused to remove your POW bracelet and our doctor finally agreed to let John wear it but it had to be taped first.

My husband and my son's father was killed fighting for what he thought was right-but we aren't bitter over our loss— instead we wish only for a lasting peace . . . .
Sincerely yours,
Ellen Hooker and Sons, Dale, John
Box 323
Heyburn, Idaho 83336

One of my favorite bracelet-wearer friends, who has continued to faithfully write me since she was twelve years old, is Kim Johnston. Part of her first letter reads:

Dear Maj. Jay Jensen:

. . . I had a POW bracelet with your name on it for a year and a few months. I saw you get off the plane at Travis Airport in the Philippines. You look great! And you are so cute, they showed a really good picture of you getting off the plane.

Some of the things that have changed here are: Entertainment, dirty movies, or for rides, Magic Mountain. Odds and

Ends stuff: Women's short dresses, men's long hair. Also Martin Luther King and Presidents Kennedy, Truman and Johnson died, so we don't have any presidents left except Nixon. Also in case you are interested, Nat King Cole died.

Love,
Your POW bracelet wearer
Kim Johnston

Kim is quite a gal isn't she? Kim's mother wrote also, and added:

Feb. 20, 1973

Major Jay R. Jensen:
    We sat here tonight viewing a wonderful sight, though it was thru tear-filled eyes. The tears were pure joy. "Happiness is having your POW released, returned home and especially seeing him."
    Our daughter, Kimberly, has worn your POW bracelet for several years. It was our prayer that you — and all the other POWs and MIAs would come home. She celebrated her 12th birthday on Feb. 10th. It was that very day that we heard you would be released from Hanoi, that made her birthday an even bigger celebration.
    Words really can't express our feelings and I've tried several times to write before this — nothing I say seems adequate to express our deepest gratitude to you and all the other POWs. Words can't express the joy we feel. Seeing you tonight was like seeing a relative or very close friend—yet we are strangers . . .
    If happiness is having people care — your cup runs over. One adorable 12-year old girl has cared very much, so has her family, friends and millions of Americans all join in "caring" It's great to have you home!

Sincerely,
Pat Johnston

You can easily see why these bracelet wearers and their letters meant so very much to me. Another letter touched my heart:

February 23, 1973
Dear Major Jensen:
Hi! You don't know me, but my name is Sara Zeigler. I'm sixteen years old and attend Richfield High School in Waco, Texas.

Over a year ago now I longed for a POW bracelet. A silver metal token with which to remember our men serving their country in Vietnam. The thought of a bracelet remained in the back of my mind all summer. Finally, in November, on my birthday, I got my wish. It was the smallest gift of all. I dared not dream what was in it! It turned out to be my favorite present — a bracelet with your name inscribed on it and the date in February, 1967, when you were to have been taken prisoner. I quickly slipped it on my arm and promised myself that I would take it off under no conditions until you once again set foot on American soil. I thought of you often. I pictured my unknown friend in a dark cell or under hard labor. I prayed for you nightly.

When I heard on the radio early one morning about a Vietnam peace agreement possibly, I was beside myself with joy! Three weeks later, it happened. And the prisoners were to come home. What happiness and hope you must have felt! I scanned the newspaper's POW list for week upon week. Finally, in a list of over 400 names, yours was one of the very last, under Utah. I felt like framing that tiny article!!

Weeks later, the first group came home. Although you were not among them, I never gave up hope.... Two days later, your name was again in the paper. Tears came to my eyes — so you really were coming back!.... The day you came home last weekend, my dreams were answered. Fearing that you might be ill or dying, I tuned in once more and found that all were in good shape.... I thanked God for your return. No, your six years of captivity were not in vain, for the great service you gave your country can only be paid with riches above. May God bless you!

Your friend, Sara Zeigler

One girl, Norma McAdam of So. Hempstead, N.Y., wrote that when I returned home she gave my POW bracelet a military funeral. However, her Boxer dog dug it up 30 minutes later.

Another young gal, Miss Kim Massie, a 15-year old sophomore from Carthage Community High in Illinois, sent my father her picture and a letter. Kim wrote:

> *I have become quite interested in the Vietnam situation, and pray for the release of all POWs . . . I received my POW bracelet on Oct. 28, 1971, and I've worn it ever since the day I put it on. I've worn this bracelet through about everything — my arm has turned green and now I have a rash on my arm, but I feel very devoted to Jay R. Jensen, so I will keep it on.*

There were many other bracelet wearers who wrote and, because of their deep feelings toward me and towards our country and its problems, will always mean a lot to me, such as Barbara Parker, Dorothy Lynch and Barbara K. Masterson. Due to the hundreds of letters such as these received by dad and me, we have come to one big conclusion — that Americans "care." They care about fellow Americans, their country and the freedom of the world. They care enough to get involved. One of the benefits occurring from the tremendous sacrifice our country has made in Vietnam is that our young people — the leaders of tomorrow — showed themselves unafraid to get emotionally concerned and involved with doing what they could to help solve the problems and struggles of our great country. Yes, the Kims, the Johns, the Saras, the young in heart and spirit of America — to me, they highlight a promise of a brighter future. Who knows, they might just be the "light at the end of the tunnel."

Chapter Seventeen

A NATION GIVES THANKS

Those weeks at March Air Force Base were hectic! The Air Force was trying desperately to help us and our families all they could. At the same time they needed to give us a very thorough physical and mental examination, completely debrief us, and help us plan our future. Of course we wanted answers to all our hundreds of questions, and we wanted to do a million and one things and make up for six years — all right now!

The Air Force treated our families just great! "Operation Homecoming" was a great success. Much of the credit at March AFB goes to Colonel George H. Fong, the homecoming team chief. Everything was very well organized and carried out, with the needs and desires of each POW the determining factor for many decisions. Immediately we were scheduled for all the medical tests, etc., we needed. Between medical appointments we were completely debriefed by specially trained and assigned briefing officers.

Debriefings

My briefing officer was Major William A. Barnett. Bill and I spent many hours debriefing. There was absolutely no pressure on us as far as what we could or should say. It was strictly a means of getting any and all information about our shoot-down, ejection, evasion (if any), capture, and all the details we could remember about our treatment, torture, conditions, food, etc. No information about another prisoner's conduct was asked for. The information we gave would be used strictly for helping the services upgrade their survival schools and training to better prepare future potential POWs.

Bill and I became good friends, along with our families. We even took our families to Disneyland together. Bill's wife Angi even consented to take me shopping for new clothes and to bring me up-to-date on the new styles. We had great fun buying me a new wardrobe. The Men's Fashion Association of America (sharing the expense with each individual store) gave each POW $500 worth of new clothes. I surely appreciated that fine gesture.

Each evening in the hospital, they would show us special films and news reviews of the past seven years to try to bring us up-to-date on all the important happenings. We were given several books too. One was a synopsis of news stories 1965-1971. Another was a book of slang expressions, so we could understand what our children and young people were talking about. We also received a special News Digest from Copley Newspapers.

Rear: Bill Yearsley; Front: Dad Jensen,
Jay, and Bill Barnett

Another escort officer had been assigned to me and my family at March Air Force Base. The Air Force was really taking good care of us and our families. His name was Major William Yearsley. I don't know what we would have done without Bill over the next few days, weeks, and months. Bill is very tall, about 6'6", thin, very personable, thoughtful, and a real "ball of fire." He has a lovely wife and family.

He met all my family, arranged transportation, rooms, showed them where to eat, briefed them on everything that was happening, gave them VIP treatment, and really made them feel at home. He took us places, ran many errands, helped me answer letters, kept track of phone calls and messages, and did a million favors for me. He did much more than expected or warranted — above and beyond the call of duty. My family and I are deeply indebted to him and his family for their unselfish kindness and friendship. We became great friends. Bill's life will never be the same after getting involved with the Jensens.

Future Assignments

Personnel from Air Force headquarters were there to talk to us, advising us on what assignments were available. We were given our choice of assignment. If a vacancy existed and we were qualified to fill the slot — it was ours. They bent over backwards to give us what we wanted and still keep the best interests of the service intact. They sought to give us future positions where we could use the valuable experience we had gained to help other Air Force personnel. Also, they wanted us to catch up with our contemporaries concerning what the Air Force had been doing the past years. Professional military schools and advanced degrees at civilian colleges were offered. Both pilot and navigator special flying recurrency programs were set up to accommodate POWs.

Pay and Leave Time

Our pay while POWs was tax free. If not already allotted, it went into the Armed Services Overseas Saving Plan at 10% interest. We had accumulated quite a bit of leave time while POWs. Normally, a serviceman cannot save or accrue more than 60 days leave, but through a special Act of Congress they allowed POWs to accrue all their leave and then we were paid for this leave time upon our return. (Normal leave accrued is 30 days a year.) In my case I would have preferred to take the leave (six months) instead of being paid the six months base pay. However I had no choice, and really no complaint either.

After our physicals and debriefing were completed (which averaged three or four weeks), we were all given 90 days convalescent leave.

Shortly after our arrival, we all received personal letters of welcome home from the President of the United States, the Secretary of Defense, the Chairman of the Joint Chiefs of Staff, the Chief of Staff of the Air Force, and others.

If we decided we wanted to get out of the service, the Air Force also assisted us in finding desired employment. As directed by the President and Department of Defense, an "Industry Committee on POW Employment" had a broad program to help POWs find jobs.

POW Gifts

There were a great number of people, associations, companies, and businesses all over the world that wanted to do things for the POWs. All such offers of gifts and assistance were closely reviewed and approved by Department of Defense. In no way could the gifts be made the object of commercial publicity or exploitation of one's personal privacy. Gifts had to comply with existing regulations concerning gifts to military personnel. Many of these tokens of appreciation were approved, and we as POWs were very grateful for them. I took advantage of many of these wonderful offers. Some of them I didn't get to take advantage of but I feel are worthy of mention are: A Caribbean cruise by Epirotiki Lines, A Key West Florida vacation, and air transportation for families within California by Pacific Southwest Airlines.

I did take advantage of the following: The loan of an Ford LTD for a year including insurance and all repair costs; Mattel toys for my family; slides of the Apollo II moon landings from movie newsreels; a lifetime pass to all major league professional baseball games, and complimentary lifetime memberships to AMVETS and European Health Spas. This is by no means a complete list.

Telephone Calls

During those weeks at March AFB Hospital, not only were we treated royally by the Air Force and hospital people, but we received hundreds of phone calls and letters each day. Special "Operation Homecoming" phone circuits were set aside for our use. I was either making or receiving at least 20 calls per day, and receiving between 30-50 letters or telegrams each day from friends, relatives, bracelet holders, and would-be friends. We were pretty busy, especially considering the slow pace to which we were accustomed.

My parents stayed in California for a week, and my children and brother and sisters stayed there five days. We had a nice family reunion party at the officers' club one night. It was also a big moment for me to be able to attend church with my parents and children. I had looked forward to that blessing for a long time.

"A Prayer Answered."
Dad, Jay, Mom, attending.
Church together, February 1973

"A precious moment."
Roger, Carrie, little 'Heidi', Jay, and Sherrie,

Brigham Young University

The Chairman of the Joint Chiefs of Staff, Admiral Thomas Moorer, was scheduled to give a talk at Brigham Young University in Provo, Utah, during their military week. Since I was a graduate of BYU, I was invited by him to attend. This was my first public appearance. The Air Force had agreed that after the POWs had completed their medical exams and debriefing the press could have a formal press interview with us. We could not have any other local interviews or give talks until after the big press interview. I was invited to BYU before I had completed my debriefing or had my big

164

*Jay's first public appearance, February, 1973, at
Brigham Young University in Provo, Utah.
Admiral Thomas Moorer, Chairman, Joint
Chiefs of Staff, Jay, ROTC Cadets, and others*

press interview. Therefore, I could not speak at BYU; but they did introduce me, and I was very honored to be there. I talked with former BYU president Ernest Wilkinson, and LDS Church Apostle Boyd K. Packer. I also attended a luncheon at Hotel Utah in Salt Lake City in connection with Admiral Moorer's visit.

While I was in Utah for this first quick visit (just two days), I did get to visit Mom and Dad at their home in Sandy, Utah. I also attended the funeral of my uncle, Ernest Pierce. Then it was back to March AFB to complete my debriefing and medical examinations.

I completed my debriefing and most of the medical exams and tests in the next few days. However, I was assigned to March AFB Hospital a few more weeks to receive some extensive dental work. The Air Force did not stop here, however. There would be another complete physical in 90 days and then an exam once each year for the next five years. All the POWs, even those out of the service, would undergo this very complete medical at Brooks AFB in Texas. Brooks is equipped to give "astronaut" physicals, and ours would be very similar.

*At Brigham Young University,
Son, Roger; President Ernest L. Wilkinson; Jay*

*A brief encounter at Brigham Young University,
"Come see me and we'll talk," was the invitation of
Elder Boyd K. Packer, an Apostle of The Church
of Jesus Christ of Latter-day Saints*

Freedom of the Press

My press interview was scheduled for Friday, 9 March 1973. It was going to be a difficult situation for me. Normally, they had scheduled at least three POWs together to face the press, but I had just missed the last one and no one else was ready. So I would be alone.

First of many press interviews

The press, represented by local California plus a few national papers, had not been friendly. Some of the reporters were very opinionated, highly critical, and not only anti-president, but antiwar. I was warned to be extremely careful in my answers, that they be very plain and simple so they could not be confused or misinterpreted. I was not censored by the Air Force at all, being free to say anything I wanted. However, because there were still POWs in the hands of the enemy, we did not want to jeopardize their release or treatment.

Therefore, we had agreed among ourselves while still captives that until all known POWs were released, we would not say anything about the bad treatment, etc. I am sure some of the reporters did not like this attitude or understand it, nor did some of them care. All they were interested in was a story that would sell or complement their own personal views. I was very disappointed with the interview. When I read an article in a newspaper the next day, I was irate. I was misquoted seven times. Some of the misquotes were very embarrassing to me and my family, such as listing my married daughter's age as 15 instead of 17. Some of the other statements I made so carefully were turned around 180 degrees to read just the opposite to what I had obviously intended. I asked the Air Force officials if I should ask for a retraction but they advised against it, saying that the reporter would really crucify me then. Our so called "freedom of the press" really means to some reporters that they are free to change or slant the facts or direct testimony they report. Some editorialize the news instead of reporting just the facts and the whole story.

A Hero's Welcome

The next day, 10 March 1973, I flew home to Salt Lake City, Utah. This was my official welcome home. When I got on the airplane, the captain offered me a bottle of champagne (only one of many I appreciated, but graciously turned down or else gave to friends). He introduced me as a VIP to the passengers.

The snow-filled mountains in Utah looked just great to me. I had really missed them. As we flew over Salt Lake City, I noticed some new landmarks in the city. It was really growing and looked beautiful to me.

After we landed the flight attendants insisted I get off the aircraft first. I was really surprised. There was a large crowd to greet me, besides all my family, relatives, and friends. A few television cameras and reporters were there too, and all in all it was a very wonderful, heartwarming homecoming.

Waiting for me at the airport was a brand new, yellow Ford LTD for my use for one year, courtesy of Larsen Ford, Murray, Utah. The owner, Park Larsen, was a very close friend of mine, and it was his idea and project to loan each POW a new Ford for one year.

I had a local press interview at the airport after the excitement had died down, and we listened to it on the radio on the way home from the airport. We also watched it on television that night. I was on another television show that evening, and several more later. As I arrived at my parent's home in Sandy, a large banner was across Main Street which said "Welcome Home Jay." All this publicity was quite unexpected by me. We did not feel that we deserved all this attention, and we felt a little embarrassed. We do not look upon ourselves as the real heroes of the war. But we received quite a welcome!

Home at last, March 1973
Dad and Jay

The Real Heroes

Then who are the real heroes of this war? They are those still missing or killed in action, those wounded or disabled — all those who served honorably in Vietnam. There were a few among us whom we considered real heroes: those who never gave up faith and resisted so many years despite torture and hardship — these are our heroes. But we all received the heroes' welcome, and we accepted that welcome, with the adulations and publicity that went with it. We accepted it for all the others, for the MIAs and KIAs. America needed Heroes.

We accept that honor in place of our fellow crewmen who were shot down, but didn't come back — those who were killed or died of torture, mistreatment, neglect or disease — or those MIAs or POWs still held captive. To these fellow comrades whom we honor, a fellow POW, Jerry Coffee, wrote this toast:

One More Roll

We toast our hearty comrades
Who have fallen from the sky,
And gently caught by God's own hand
to be with Him on high.

To dwell among the soaring clouds
They knew so well before,
From dawn patrol to victory roll
At heaven's very door.

And as we fly among them there
We are sure to hear their plea —
"Take care my friend, watch your six,
and do one more roll — just for me."

We accept publicity, and we give speeches and talks and interviews because we feel we have a message to give the American people. I believe we have a message for all Americans — That Courage, Honor, and Faith conquer any adversity, and solve any problem. As prisoners we gained far greater love for our country, appreciation for its freedoms, blessings, opportunities, and our high standard of living. Yes, we experienced the true meaning of the phrase "America the Beautiful." Oh, I know our country isn't perfect, our government isn't perfect, but it is the closest to perfection in the world.

Survival, Honor, and Service

I have often been asked, "How did you get through the ordeal? What was the biggest help to you?" The biggest help to me came from within: my military training, education, parents, and my church. But most important was my faith and testimony in God, faith in my country, faith in my family, and faith in the American people.

When I was a young Boy Scout I remember taking an oath and resolving that, "On my honor, I will do my best, to do my duty to God and my country. . . . " I have always tried to live up to that oath. I have sometimes failed, but I kept trying — to the best of my ability. As I grew older I realized there was someone else we must serve besides God and country. We must serve our families, our parents, our brothers and sisters. Later on, I realized that we must serve our spouse, and children. When I went to Vietnam I realized there were others we must serve: our brothers, our fellowmen — all mankind. And that is the reason that I served so proudly in Vietnam, and will serve in any other country in the future that needs us to help them preserve their freedom. Those six years I thought about this very deeply, and I decided that I would take that oath again and I hope that you will join me — that all America will join me — in resolving that "On our honor, we will do our best, to do our duty to God, country, our family, and all mankind." May God bless us and help us to do so.

171

Note: *Please xerox this page for your order form*

P.O.W.
(Publications of Worth)
P.O. Box 2080
Orcutt, CA 93455
(805) 937-0869

Books	Price	Quan.	Cost
Six Years in Hell	$10.00		
Vietnam — Lessons Learned*	10.00		
America — Decay from Within**	10.00		

Booklets

	Price	Quan.	Cost
Leadership — Traits & Principles	$3.00		
The Art of Delegating	3.00		
Becoming an Effective Speaker	3.00		
How Much are You Worth?	3.00		
A Family Budget Made Simple	3.00		
How to Choose a Wife*	3.00		

Tapes

	Price	Quan.	Cost
Six Years in Hell (audio book) (270 minutes on 3 audio cassettes)	$20.00		
Conquering Adversity (audio) (60-minute audio cassette of talk)	10.00		
Conquering Adversity (video-vhs) (60-minute video tape of talk)	30.00		

Sub-total			
California Residents: add 6% sales tax			
UPS Shipping: $1.50 per item, $3.00 max			

TOTAL AMOUNT ENCLOSED $ _____

SHIP TO: _____

NAME

_____

ADDRESS

_____

CITY   STATE   ZIP

Autograph to: _____

Check if Speaker Information Package Desired _____

*Estimated Printing Date is March, 1990
**Estimated Printing Date is September, 1990